Scott Joplin

COMPOSER

Black Americans of Achievement

L E G A C Y   E D I T I O N

Black Americans of Achievement

LEGACY EDITION

Scott Joplin

COMPOSER

Janet Hubbard-Brown

CHELSEA HOUSE
PUBLISHERS
An imprint of Infobase Publishing

Scott Joplin

Copyright © 2006 by Infobase Publishing

Chelsea House
An imprint of Infobase Publishing
132 West 31st Street
New York NY 10001

Library of Congress Cataloging-in-Publication Data
Hubbard-Brown, Janet.
    Scott Joplin / Janet Hubbard-Brown.— Legacy ed.
        p. cm.— (Black Americans of achievement)
    "Compositions of Scott Joplin": p. .
Includes bibliographical references (p.) and index.
ISBN 0-7910-9211-9 (hardcover)
1. Joplin, Scott, 1868–1917—Juvenile literature. 2. Composers—United States—
Biography—Juvenile literature. 3. Ragtime music—History and criticism—Juvenile
literature. I. Title. II. Series.
ML3930.J66H83 2006
780.92—dc22   2006004435

Chelsea House books are available at special discounts when purchased in bulk quantities
for businesses, associations, institutions, or sales promotions. Please call our Special Sales
Department in New York at (212) 967-8800 or (800) 322-8755.

You can find Chelsea House on the World Wide Web at
http://www.chelseahouse.com

Series and cover design by Keith Trego, Takeshi Takahashi

Printed in the United States of America

Bang Hermitage 10 9 8 7 6 5 4 3 2 1

Contents

"Maple Leaf Rag"– Ragtime's Biggest Hit

When a quiet-natured African American in his mid-20s named Scott Joplin arrived in Sedalia, Missouri, in 1894, it seemed that everyone in the town was passionate about music, in one form or another. Bands marched through the streets playing military and minstrel music. Dances were held on a regular basis. March music wasn't just martial music; it was fun to dance to, as well. People danced the two-step and the polka to marching songs. Operas and operettas, minstrel shows, concerts, and recitals were well-attended. A variety of quartets performed around town.

Beatrice Martin, a lifelong resident of Sedalia, said, "Sedalia has been nothing but music…. All my life this was called the 'musical town of the West.'"

Alexander Graham Bell and Thomas Edison were working on the development of the phonograph at the time, but until 1915, when the "talking machine" became more affordable, people made their own music. Children learned to play instruments, the piano and the guitar being favorites. Most homes had a piano, and most families had at least one member who could play it with some skill. When families and friends gathered, it was not unusual for someone to bring along a stack of sheet music to sing or play. White people were drawn to waltzes, polkas, quadrilles, reels, and marches. Blacks were more accustomed to folk songs, spirituals, and blues.

A NEW SOUND

African-American musicians were coming up with a new sound that had a tremendous energy. It combined the European marches with the music they played and listened to on plantations. This sound poured out of clubs and dance halls on Sedalia's Main Street. What set it apart from other music was its syncopated, or ragged, rhythm. When a white newspaper critic heard it, he referred to it as "rag time." The phrase, though, had been bandied about for years.

The music was lilting and jaunty, and the lyrics to many of the songs were considered vulgar by some people. As its popularity increased, it created controversy, much the way rock 'n' roll would over a half-century later when Elvis Presley appeared on television. Compared with the traditional and sentimental music Americans were used to hearing, ragtime felt wild and uninhibited. Joplin had been spellbound by it at the Chicago World's Fair in 1893, when it started to catch on

IN HIS OWN WORDS...

Scott Joplin was asked by a writer from the *American Musician and Art Journal* why he called his style of music "ragtime." Joplin replied:

Oh! Because it has such a ragged movement. It suggests something like that.

Scott Joplin was one of the originators of ragtime music, which first became popular in the 1890s. Compared with the music of the time, ragtime seemed wild and uninhibited. Joplin would spend much of his career trying to elevate ragtime to a serious art.

with the American public. He had studied classical music when he was a boy, and he had also been greatly shaped by the music he heard at home, in the church, and in the fields and saloons. These influences made him a natural when it came to composing and playing ragtime.

Sedalia, like much of the United States, was segregated. But African Americans and whites mingled more comfortably there than in other parts of the country. Clubs were popular in both the black and white communities, and it wasn't uncommon for whites to attend events at the black clubs. In 1898, an African-American man named Tony Williams—an extraordinary dancer and musician—established the Black 400 Club, which required membership. The Maple Leaf Club, another club for blacks, was also incorporated on Main Street. That street was often referred to as "Battle Row" because of the 35 saloons, gambling halls, dance halls, and brothels that lined it. Williams hired Joplin to sing and play piano.

Some musicians playing ragtime at those clubs, including Joplin, were trying to write down their compositions and sell them to publishing houses. Sheet music was at the heart of the music industry. For new composers, having a song published was crucial to its success. Because of prejudice, however, an African American had a much harder time trying to sell his music than a white composer would. In 1897, Joplin's friend Tom Turpin became the first black ragtime composer to sell his work, a song called "Harlem Rag."

Joplin had sold a couple of his compositions for a flat fee of $25 each. He had had no luck, though, in selling an instrumental piece called "Maple Leaf Rag," which he felt was his best work to date. It had been rejected twice, and he was worried.

SELLING THE "MAPLE LEAF RAG"

That was when fate stepped in. A white gentleman named John Stark, who liked to sell and tune pianos, owned a local music store. He had come to Sedalia from Chillicothe, Missouri, in 1885 to open the store with his son, William. Before that, he had been selling ice cream and reed organs to farm families. He was a businessman always on the lookout for a way to make money to support his family. Stark was born a Southerner, but during the Civil War he had sympathized with Northerners. He married a Southern woman, and they had three children. Black culture intrigued him, and he liked to play black folk songs on his guitar. Once he had established his store in Sedalia, he liked to invite local musicians to come and perform there. He also kept a large stock of sheet music. It was a great source of pride to him in his later years that two of his children became accomplished musicians.

In one version of the story on how Joplin sold "Maple Leaf Rag," John Stark entered a club one afternoon and heard Joplin playing his latest composition. Stark drank a beer and told Joplin to bring the music to his store the next day. A business contract was signed, and Joplin was on his way.

The report of Stark's son, William, however, placed the two men in his father's office. He said that after his father listened to Joplin play, Stark told him he thought the piece was too difficult for amateurs to learn. Joplin asked Stark: If he brought someone in off the street, and that person could play it, would Stark publish the work? Stark agreed. Joplin went out and brought back a teenage African-American male who sat down and played the song perfectly. Stark kept his promise. William Stark believed that Joplin had been coaching the youth for months.

William Stark's wife gave a different version. She said that Joplin walked into the Stark store with the "Maple Leaf Rag" manuscript in one hand and the hand of a little African-American boy in the other. He played, and the boy danced. John Stark thought that no one would play the song because of its difficulty, but William Stark was so impressed that he decided to publish the music.

A final version is that a lawyer named R. A. Higdon stepped in and helped Joplin sell his music to Stark. Each story probably contains a grain of truth. What matters, though, is that John Stark did obtain the rights to "Maple Leaf Rag." Whether

With the sale of the rights for "Maple Leaf Rag" to John Stark, Scott Joplin received a one-cent-per-copy royalty. At the time, a black composer rarely, if ever, earned royalties. In an era before the phonograph became affordable, the publishing of sheet music was crucial to a song's success.

Joplin made his own deal or had a lawyer help him, the end result was that Joplin was to receive a one-cent-per-copy royalty, ten free copies, and the right to buy additional copies for five cents each. It was unheard of at the time for a black musician to earn royalties. For the first time, Joplin would have some financial freedom. But more than that, "Maple Leaf

Rag" helped create a decade-long fad that took the country by storm.

Joplin's peers, and later, his biographers, were in awe of his talent. Jelly Roll Morton, the famous jazz pianist of New Orleans, called Joplin "the greatest ragtime writer who ever lived."

Pianist and composer J. Russell Robinson said, "I think it ['Maple Leaf Rag'] is one of the finest tunes ever written … the King of Rags, and in my way of thinking, nothing that Joplin or any other rag writers wrote ever came close to it."

Joplin's biographer, Edward A. Berlin, wrote, "There was no rag that could compare with it in terms of rhythmic vitality, imagination, and originality.… With the 'Maple Leaf Rag,' Joplin's career took a giant leap forward, and ragtime entered a new age."

Scott Joplin's tunes would have a huge influence on American music for years to come. But he would also learn that fame was fleeting, and his quest to elevate ragtime to the realm of serious art would occupy the rest of his life.

2

The Texas Frontier

Scott Joplin's exact birth date is not known. He was born in northeastern Texas, and his birth date is often given as November 24, 1868. Census records, though, certify that on June 1, 1870, he was already two years old. It could be said that modern American culture took shape between his birth and his death. His father, Giles, was born in North Carolina around 1842 into a family of slaves. Charles Moores, the slaveholder, brought Giles to Texas from South Carolina in 1850 and freed him in the late 1850s before the Emancipation Proclamation was issued. It was said that Giles played the fiddle at dances held at his master's household. After Giles was freed, he took up farming.

Scott's mother, Florence Givens, was freeborn in Kentucky around 1841 and traveled with her father and grandmother to Texas before the Civil War. There, in Cass County, she met Giles Joplin, and they were married in 1860. Scott had an older brother, Monroe, who was born during the Civil War. Another brother, Robert, was born a year after Scott. The birth of three more siblings followed.

WAR AND RECONSTRUCTION

Close to 200,000 slaves from all over the South had settled in Texas by 1861. No major battles of the Civil War were fought in that state. The white farmers and planters, whose chief crops were cotton and lumber, were basically unaffected by the war, until the South lost in 1865. The long, hard process of rebuilding the country, called Reconstruction, had barely begun. Though circumstances seemed to be better for blacks after the war, a fundamental truth about Reconstruction America in the last three decades of the nineteenth century was that "freedom of movement, artistic expression, and economic opportunities could all be cut short by lynch mobs, discriminatory booking practices, and Jim Crow laws." Unlike the rest of the South, the war did not leave Texas in ruins. Many Texans resisted Reconstruction and wanted to hold onto the old social system. Texas was the second-to-last state to be readmitted to the Union under the plan to reconstruct the nation. Finally, in 1870, Texas grudgingly granted citizenship to all former slaves. Eventually, tensions eased somewhat, and Texas became known to freedmen and freedwomen as a good place to start a new life.

Still, race relations were confusing; though the slaves were free, old attitudes were in place on both sides. Many whites still expected blacks to work for free, and blacks were uncertain what their new freedom meant. Whites were fearful that the former slaves would try to take over, and that fear made them fight the efforts made by blacks to establish themselves. Whites owned the businesses and the land, which put blacks in the position of having to seek work from them. Some of these owners quickly adapted to the changes taking place and offered employment to their African-American neighbors, but

An 1867 illustration from *Harper's Weekly* shows African-American men voting in a state election in the South. In the Reconstruction states that year, 703,000 blacks and 627,000 whites voted. Although circumstances for blacks were better after the Civil War, they still faced threats to their freedom—ranging from Jim Crow laws and discriminatory practices to lynch mobs.

others were not so forthcoming. Other problems existed. Slaves had received little or no education, and their inability to read or write put them at a great disadvantage.

This was the atmosphere in which Scott Joplin was raised. Fortunately, his parents and many of their neighbors were determined to thrive in a new environment. Even in the face of hostility, they forged new lives. They saw that they could earn a living with hard work. One positive legacy of the old plantation life was a rich cultural heritage, with music at its center. The deeply burdened slaves sang the blues, but much of their music was joyous and involved singing, clapping, and dancing. Workers on the railroad chanted, and women washing laundry sang.

MUSIC IN THE FAMILY

Like many of their neighbors, members of the Joplin family were musical. Florence sang and played the banjo, and Giles, who had been in a plantation orchestra during his slave years, played the violin. Scott, Robert, and their younger brother William also played the violin, and Scott was playing banjo by the time he was seven years old. They had not yet been exposed to the piano, which was too expensive for most families. Besides Scott, Robert and William would eventually become professional musicians, too.

The presence of a large black community would prove to be crucial to the brothers' musical development, because it allowed them to become familiar with the African and Afro-American rhythms and sounds that would eventually be incorporated into ragtime. Joplin must have been exposed to a variety of melodies, rhythms, and traditions from all across the South, including New Orleans.

The Joplins moved several times shortly after Scott's birth— first to Linden, Texas, and then to Jefferson, Texas—in search of better living conditions. Across the country, a movement from farming to industrialization was taking place. Giles Joplin decided to move again when he heard that the railroad was hiring men in Texarkana, a bustling frontier town on the Texas–Arkansas border some 30 miles north of Louisiana. The town was being developed around the junction of two major railroad lines, the Texas and Pacific Railroad and the Cairo and

Fulton Line. Legend has it that the railroad surveyor who was sent to choose the site for the junction marked the place with a wooden sign containing three letters from the name of each nearby state: TEX-ARK-ANA.

Most of the newcomers in Texarkana were whites who had left their homes in Alabama, Georgia, Mississippi, and the Carolinas, but because of the available work, the town also attracted a large black population. The move was an adjustment for the Joplins, who were coming to the city from the country. On the positive side, white and black railroad

The Role of Trains in Ragtime

In the minds of many, the train was a symbol of the transition from a rural, agricultural past to an urban life. This was particularly true for blacks, whose primary method of transportation out of the South was the train. Traveling shows also toured by rail, and there are stories of blacks who stowed away in boxcars, creating music as they went. One of Scott Joplin's early compositions was "The Great Crush Collision March," which he dedicated to the Missouri, Kansas & Texas Railway.

The steady rhythm of trains became a part of black music, including ragtime and later jazz. Susan Curtis, the author of *Dancing to a Black Man's Tune: A Life of Scott Joplin*, wrote, "The steady beat of the left hand [in ragtime] echoed the rhythm of factory, machine, and train, but the unexpected accents by the right hand, as well as the fast-paced melodies, announced a refusal to be contained by that steadiness."

Luther G. Williams wrote, "The left hand [in ragtime] defined the beat and the harmonies." He went on to say that that beat could have been taken from factory work, the assembly line, the printing press, domestic labor, and dancing. And, of course, the train.

Joplin wrote "The Great Crush Collision March" in 1896 after seeing a planned head-on collision that destroyed two locomotives in September of that year near Waco, Texas. William Crush, a railroad official, staged the collision as a public-relations stunt to get farmers and railroaders to stop feuding. The event ended in tragedy when the boilers on the two 35-ton locomotives exploded, killing three spectators among the 50,000 in attendance and injuring many others.

employees were paid the same salary, and the coming and going of trains brought residents and workers in contact with people, goods, and music from all parts of the country.

Giles rented a small house in the black section of town, where Florence took in laundry. They wanted their children to have an education because they knew it was the key to true freedom. There were hurdles to overcome. The public school system was just being established amid opposition from people who did not want their tax dollars used to pay for the education of other people's children. Opposition to schools for black children was particularly strong. It was not uncommon for the few schools set up for blacks in the South to be burned down and for the teachers who taught in these schools to be horsewhipped and run out of town. Scott's parents, like many of their neighbors, arranged for their children to be taught by the literate adults in the black community. According to the 1880 U.S. census, Scott and his brother Robert were attending school, and their sister Osie went occasionally. All could read, as could their father and their brother, Monroe.

Giles Joplin did not want to encourage Scott's interest in music too much, because he believed that it was almost impossible to earn a decent living as a musician. Scott's mother had a different opinion, and when she began working for white families as a cleaning lady, she made sure that her most talented son was allowed to tag along and play her employers' pianos while she worked. These differences may have been a source of friction between his parents. Scott was so musically gifted, in fact, that music teachers in the community quickly began to notice his talent. Several offered to teach him without charge. Mag Washington was one. J. C. Johnson was another. Johnson was a neighbor who worked as a barber, a real estate dealer, and a teacher. Dubbed "the professor," he taught piano, violin, and horn. He taught Scott how to read music and how to play the piano, and he played piano arrangements of the great instrumental and operatic compositions of Europe for

Scott. (Scott was soon able to compose his own music and to improvise.)

It was a German immigrant named Julius Weiss, however, who probably had the biggest influence on the young musician. Weiss was a private tutor for the children of a founding landowner in Texarkana, and when he could, he taught other children in town. He offered to teach Scott for free. Through Weiss, Scott began to see music as an art, as well as entertainment.

When he was 12 or 13, Scott's father left home to live with another woman. It must have been devastating for Florence and her children. Florence took over the household, supporting her family with domestic work. Monroe had already left home. Florence moved the family to less expensive housing. Somehow, she managed to buy a piano for Scott. All the money he earned doing odd jobs went to buy sheet music, which generally cost five or ten cents.

YOUNG AND TALENTED

Scott soon earned a reputation in the black and the white communities as a talented young musician. An old family neighbor would recall many years later that Scott "was smart, especially in music.... He did not have to play anybody else's music. He made up his own, and it was beautiful! He just got his music out of the air."

Scott's determination to succeed as a musician may have stemmed in part from his lack of alternatives. For a young black man in Texarkana in the 1880s, few career opportunities were available. He could be a manual laborer for the railroad, the sawmill, or the lumber camp; a servant in a white household; or a preacher or teacher, all poorly paid. Scott knew that his musical ability gave him an option that most of his peers did not have, and he was determined to make the most of this opportunity.

A former neighbor would later say, "Scott was earnest. When a bunch of boys got together on a spree one night and asked Scott to go with them, he said, 'No sir, I won't have any-thing to do with such foolishness. I'm going to make a man out of myself.'"

By the time Scott was in his mid- to late teens, he had achieved moderate success as a musician in his hometown. His mother had died, however, and he was aware that an exciting world was waiting for a young and talented musician. For the first time, it was possible to take a train from Texarkana to Dal-las, Memphis, and St. Louis, to name a few places.

The westward expansion, one of the greatest migrations in the history of mankind, had a tremendous impact on the lives of the people in the Midwestern part of the United States. To some of them, it seemed as if the entire country was on the move as people gave up their homes in the older, more settled parts of the East and headed west. Traveling however they could—by riding mules and horses, driving teams of oxen hitched to wagons, riding on steamboats and in railroad cars—they were lured by the promise of free or inexpensive land and the chance to start over and get ahead.

Besides the influx of settlers, there were also thousands of other itinerants traveling across the countryside: businessmen, land speculators, fortune hunters, and entertainers. Traveling among them were hundreds of musicians who wandered from town to town. Some had classical training; others could play their instruments by ear only. Some were young; others were old. Some were Europeans who had come to the United States to seek their fortunes; others were homegrown Americans. Many were white, and some were black. A number of these musicians went from town to town, sometimes as part of a traveling theatrical troupe or a minstrel show, sometimes with just another musician or two. Otherwise, they traveled alone.

ON THE ROAD

Though no records exist of this period of his life, it is thought that Joplin traveled as a "honky-tonk" pianist through Texas,

Louisiana, Missouri, Illinois, Ohio, and Kentucky, and composed music in his spare time. When a musician arrived at a new town in the late 1880s, it was relatively easy for him—especially if he was a skilled and reliable pianist—to find a job. The piano was then the most popular instrument, and the American public was eager to hear live music. Jobs for pianists were often available in saloons, restaurants, pool halls, stores and theaters. Musicians were also hired to play on steamboats and at parties, dances, picnics, horse races, and county fairs.

This photograph shows Broadway north of Chestnut Street in St. Louis, around 1890. The city's Chestnut Valley section, with Chestnut Street as one of its boundaries, was known for its nightlife. Scott Joplin spent some time there in 1890 and became friendly with Tom Turpin, a fellow composer who wrote "Harlem Rag." In the years before his stay in St. Louis, Joplin is believed to have been a "honky-tonk" pianist who traveled across the South.

Joplin spent some time during 1890 in St. Louis, where he became close to the Turpin family. St. Louis is on the brown, wide, and powerful Mississippi River, which was home to all kinds of vessels, including majestic paddle-wheel steamboats. The city had a well-known nightlife area full of cafes, saloons, boardinghouses, and brothels. This area, which was called Chestnut Valley because one of its boundaries was Chestnut Street, was considered the underside of St. Louis—the neighborhood that respectable people did not visit, even though they knew it existed. Musicians from all over the Midwest were drawn to Chestnut Valley, for there was money to be made and work to be had.

Joplin and Tom Turpin, who was a composer and pianist like Joplin, were kindred spirits. They made an interesting pair. Turpin was large and burly, while Joplin was slightly built. Joplin was also very quiet; he rarely spoke above a whisper. And he was plain and neat in his dress—unlike many of the people who performed in saloons and wore loud outfits, which might include a checkered suit, a bright silk shirt, and a patterned tie.

During this period, Joplin constantly worked on developing his own style of piano playing while he listened to the songs and styles of other pianists. He gave little thought to writing down his compositions and trying to get them published, even though his friends urged him to do so. He believed that his chances of getting published were so slim that it was hardly worth the effort. Not only was he a black musician who existed on the fringes of society, but the music he played and wrote was not considered very respectable.

The World's Fair in Chicago would help him realize that he did have a chance.

3

A Turning Point

In 1893, Scott Joplin and some of his musician friends showed up at the World's Fair in Chicago looking for work. They were amazed, like everyone else, by the electric lights and the towering Ferris wheel.

Twenty-seven million Americans attended the Chicago World's Fair, which commemorated the four-hundredth anniversary of Christopher Columbus's arrival in the New World and was officially called the World's Columbian Exposition. The fair was a turning point in Joplin's life. While there, he met many other musicians from all over the country who were also experimenting with ragtime music. Also important was his exposure to black music as well as to black musicians, who performed before white audiences and were treated with respect.

It is not known if the new ragtime music was actually played at the fair, but it was played in saloons and sporting

The Ferris wheel—the world's first—loomed large in 1893 over the World's Fair in Chicago, also known as the World's Columbian Exposition. Scott Joplin went to Chicago for the fair with some of his musician friends. Ragtime was played in the saloons near the fairgrounds and soon became popular among a wider audience. The opportunity to hear this music must have given Joplin ideas about what he could do as a musician.

houses surrounding it. Ragtime caught on quickly in Chicago, moving out of the black culture to a wider audience. Joplin was still a bit player, but his head must have been filled with dreams of what was possible. With this new music, there was always a steady beat in the bass, played by the pianist with his left hand. The right hand played the melody. The strong accents in the melody were placed so that they deliberately fell on the weak beats established by the steady rhythm of the left hand. The music was easy to dance to but was difficult to learn to play.

It was common for touring musicians to trade tunes, compare notes, and borrow melodies and techniques from one another. A gospel tune might be combined with a melody from musical theater. A classical composition might be mixed into a song from a minstrel show. While Joplin was in Chicago, he formed a band consisting (as far as we know) of a cornet, a clarinet, a tuba, and a baritone horn. He arranged pieces for the band, which performed whenever it could find employment around the fairgrounds or in Chicago's red-light district. His work with the band allowed him to try his hand at writing out the musical parts for each of the instruments. This experience would prove to be quite valuable once he began to work on his own compositions. Among the many musicians Joplin met in Chicago was Otis Saunders, a 22-year-old pianist and composer who was visiting the fair from his home in Springfield, Missouri. The two became close friends.

IN HIS OWN WORDS...

When Scott Joplin was interviewed by a *New York Age* reporter named Lester Walton in 1913 about ragtime and its growing acceptance, he commented:

There has been ragtime music in America ever since the Negro race has been here, but the white people took no notice of it until about twenty years ago.

GOOD TIMES, AND BAD

Two contrasting dynamics were happening in the country. The Gay Nineties, a phrase that was coined in the 1920s by an artist named Richard V. Culter, referred to the high life experienced by society people in New York and Boston during the last decade of the nineteenth century. For industrialists especially, the period was one of tremendous economic expansion. As much as the World's Fair was organized to reflect the progress of a vital and vast country, however, it could not hide the fact that the times were much harder for the working class. The transition from a rural and agricultural life to a more industrial and urban one had created a major shift in American culture. People who worked longer hours were having a difficult time making ends meet. There were plenty of business closings, unemployment, and bank failures in 1893. A new wave of immigrants had entered the country and lived in poverty. People were losing faith in the adage that hard work brought financial reward.

A subtle transition was occurring in the American psyche. People were gradually leaving behind the old Victorian morality that had been dominant for decades. The term *Victorian* referred to Queen Victoria of Great Britain, whose strictness about everything from clothes to morals had a big influence on the people of Great Britain and the United States. At the end of her reign, though, things began to change. College-educated women were becoming more independent. Nightlife was popular. The arts were changing, too, with a focus being placed on reality. Novels depicted downtrodden characters. Painters were choosing gritty subjects, like urban landscapes. Ragtime was the perfect accompaniment for people wanting to shuck their more old-fashioned beliefs, for it was all about being spontaneous and demonstrating joy and a lack of inhibition.

American composers were looking for an authentic American music. It is interesting that they turned to plantation songs and American Indian music for inspiration. Another genre of

Black-Face Minstrels and "Coon Songs"

The forerunner to ragtime was a type of song known as "coon songs." Going back as far as 1848, these songs were featured in minstrel shows. "Coon" was but one of many demeaning epithets bestowed on blacks. Two images of African Americans emerged from these songs, according to authors Rudi Blesh and Harriet Janis, who wrote *They All Played Ragtime*: "One was the good-hearted simpleton, loose-jointed, shuffling, and awkward, who could break into an intricate buck and wing or make the banjo talk. The other was the Negro dandy, who wore the habiliments and the customs of his 'white' superiors so absurdly." The songs were loved by white Americans.

Eventually, white performers appeared onstage with blackened faces. They wanted to present funny stories about African-American life through music, dance, and dialogue. Later, after the Civil War, black performers made their faces even darker and, following in the steps of the white performers, presented themselves as naïve, unable to speak English properly, and slow-witted, but with the ability to dance well. Often, the only opportunities available to blacks within national theater circuits involved performing caricatures. Unfortunately, these portrayals served to reinforce many whites' opinions of blacks. On the other hand, great black musical theater emerged from these shows.

Political correctness in language was not even a concept during the era of ragtime. Coon songs fell into this category. Some blacks thought the self-mockery funny, and newspapers of the time referred to "coon songs" as if it were a common term. Scott Joplin joined in, forming a drama company to put on his ballet of African-American dances. The lyrics to *The Ragtime Dance* include:

> I attended a ball last Thursday night
> Given by the dark town swells.
> Ev'ry coon came out in full dress alright
> and the girls were society belles.

The all-black Queen City Cornet Band performed a song called "Coon! Coon! Coon!" in Sedalia, and a black composer named Ernest Hogan wrote a song called "All Coons Look Alike to Me." Joplin would one day speak out against the coon songs, and although Hogan's song provided him financial security, he also regretted his contribution to this genre of music.

music that was popular for a few years were the "coon songs." They were being performed in the 1890s in early vaudeville shows. The intent was to present satire, but these performances by whites were demeaning representations of blacks and created more prejudice.

IN SEDALIA

In 1894, Joplin and Otis Saunders left Chicago together and headed to St. Louis, where they stayed with the Turpins. From there, they went to Sedalia, in central Missouri, 190 miles west of St. Louis. Joplin's brothers, Will and Robert, both of them musicians, were in Sedalia as well.

During the Civil War, Sedalia had been a Union military post, mainly because its founder, General George Radeen Smith, opposed slavery. Though the town was not without prejudice, it was more accepting of blacks than the average place of the time. Most neighborhoods included people of both races, though blacks had their own seating area in theaters, and many restaurants and saloons did not accept black customers. African Americans were able to own their own businesses and have their own churches and organizations, and they were allowed to vote. But whites continued to hold the power locally and nationally.

The population of Sedalia had risen from 4,500 in 1868 to 14,000 by 1890. It was a center of commerce and transportation. Many out-of-towners came there to do business. A prosperous town, Sedalia had 7 public schools for whites and one for blacks, 20 churches (2 for blacks), 5 newspapers, 9 banks, and 2 baseball teams. The George R. Smith College for Negroes had opened its doors. It was also known for the red-light district on Main Street, where all the saloons and houses of ill repute were located. From time to time, the more upright citizens, both blacks and whites, complained, but usually they were at least temporarily appeased. Ragtime was associated with that area of town, which, unfortunately, caused many people to turn against the music.

Sedalia's founder had set aside a section of the city for the freed blacks, which they called Lincolnville, after President Abraham Lincoln. Probably 10 percent of the population was black, the majority of them ages 18 to 44. Joplin and Saunders fit well into this vibrant black community. Though racial discrimination was still a problem, the two young men were able to be active in the social and cultural life of Sedalia.

Joplin was not allowed to join the all-white Second Regiment Band, so he joined the all-black Queen City Cornet Band. The band was formed in 1891, and its membership was constantly changing as musicians came and went. The 12-piece band, later called the Queen City Concert Band, was asked to play everywhere in the area once it became popular.

John Philip Sousa and Marches

In the late nineteenth century, as ragtime was becoming popular, brass bands were as common in America as apple pie. In 1889, there were more than 10,000 military bands in the country. Brass bands paraded on Main Streets and provided background for ice- and roller-skating, as well as weddings. Dancers preferred the march, with its regular rhythm, over the waltz. The famous dance, the fox-trot, was created to be danced to this music.

John Philip Sousa (1854–1932), who composed 136 marches, was called the "March King." As a youth, he studied violin and harmony and became an apprentice to the U.S. Marine Band. He conducted orchestras for theater productions early in his career and then became the conductor of the U.S. Marine Band from 1880 to 1892. That year, he formed Sousa's New Marine Band (later called the Sousa Band). He and his band toured the United States, Canada, Europe, and other parts of world. Some of his most famous marches include "Semper Fidelis," "The Washington Post March," and "The Stars and Stripes Forever." He also composed several comic operas.

The recording industry, which was in its first stages in the 1890s, was helped a great deal by the U.S. Marine Band, Gilmore's Band, and the Sousa Band. They were the first "recording" stars. More than 1,000 recordings were made of the Sousa Band, even though Sousa hated the new industry. He worried that it might take work away from musicians.

Under the leadership of conductor John Philip Sousa (center), the U.S. Marine Band prepares to play, in this photograph from 1890. Brass and military bands were at their height of popularity around this time, and Sousa was known as the March King.

Joplin joined soon after he arrived in Sedalia, but a couple of years later, he formed his own band of six members. The instruments he wanted were a cornet, a clarinet, an E-flat tuba, a baritone, drums, and of course, the piano.

A decade before, when he was 16, Joplin had formed his first musical group, a vocal quartet. The group was a vocal ensemble made up of Scott, his brother Will, and two neighborhood boys. Vocal quartets usually consisted of a first tenor, which was the highest pitch, a second tenor, considered the leading voice, a baritone, and a bass. The quartet's first engagement was in Clarksville, Texas, a town about 65 miles west of Texarkana, and it was a resounding success.

VOCALISTS ON TOUR

Now Joplin wanted to tour again, and in 1894 he set out with a new vocal group, his Texas Medley Quartette, which consisted of eight members, making it a double quartet. Joplin's brothers Will and Robert were a part of it. After several rehearsals, the group went on the road. The ensemble was successful enough to attract a management agency, the Majestic Booking Agency, which arranged the tours. The group's first trip took it as far east as Syracuse, New York. In 1895 and 1896, the group toured all over Missouri, Texas, Oklahoma, and Kansas, performing medleys of popular songs and plantation tunes like Stephen Foster's "Old Folks at Home," "My Old Kentucky Home," and "Camptown Races."

The ensemble also performed songs that Joplin had written. Because he had to teach his songs to the members of the Texas Medley Quartette, the easiest way for him to do this was to write down the songs. Toward the end of 1895, when the group was performing in Syracuse, he approached some local publishers with his songs. Two of his compositions—sentimental songs written in a popular style—were accepted. M. L. Mantell published "Please Say You Will," and the Leiter Brothers published "A Picture of Her Face." He was creating songs that fit the public taste. They were sentimental ballads that some referred to as "tearjerkers." These songs were designed to stir up the emotions, and for many years, they were considered the most popular music in America.

Encouraged by the acceptance of these songs, which were issued in sheet music identifying the composer as a member of the Texas Medley Quartette, Joplin decided to put onto paper more of the many pieces he had composed. In 1896, three more of his works were published in Texas. These three compositions, a waltz and two marches, were not songs with lyrics, but instrumental pieces written for the piano. All five of Joplin's earliest published compositions were standard works of the period. None of them achieved much success, nor did any of them give a hint of what was to come. These five compositions, however, were a very encouraging start for the young composer, who was about to trade his life on the road for a more stable lifestyle.

The Texas Medley Quartette ended its final tour in Joplin, Missouri, in 1897 and then disbanded. Joplin headed back with Otis Saunders to Sedalia, where he wanted to focus on composing, entertaining, and teaching.

4

Ragtime Takes Off

While Scott Joplin was establishing his reputation in Sedalia, ragtime was beginning to gain acceptance throughout the country among whites as well as blacks. An article appeared in a publication called *The Metronome* that claimed that ragtime was "of Negro origin" and "wildly popular." The writer added, "People in every grade of society have caught the fever and are calling for this class of music."

It was getting so a person could walk down any residential street in Sedalia—or in almost any other small town in America—and hear strains of ragtime being played on a piano in a house across the lawn. Although bands were still playing marches as well as other popular kinds of music, the jaunty, syncopated rhythm that is the hallmark of ragtime was beginning to creep into their renditions.

A Chicago publisher released what it claimed was the first piece of true ragtime sheet music in 1897. It was called

"Mississippi Rag" and was written by the white Chicago band-leader William H. Krell. Joplin's African-American friend Tom Turpin followed behind with his "Harlem Rag," released in December 1897. Joplin persuaded a Kansas City publisher named Carl Hoffman to accept a tune called "Original Rags" during that time, although the publisher did not release the composition until 1899. He was busy at work on "Maple Leaf Rag," too. A publisher generally bought a composition out-right from a composer for a fee of $25 to $50. No royalties were paid to the composer for each piece of his music that sold, so the publisher would get to pocket all of the profits—if there were any. Most itinerant musicians made their money from tips.

MUSIC, MUSIC, MUSIC

What was important to Joplin was that he was completely immersed in music, whether he was playing piano, organizing new bands, composing, or teaching. He also decided during this time to become a student at George R. Smith College in Sedalia. Whether he intended to study music there cannot be deter-mined, because the college's records were destroyed in a fire.

He continued to play with his smaller band, entertaining at parties, dances, socials, and get-togethers in Sedalia's black community. He also sang in quartets and played solo piano at social gatherings. These performances were considered to be much more respectable work than playing in a saloon in a red-light district. The money was not enough to support him, however, so he continued to work in saloons on a regular basis. He had little trouble moving back and forth between the two kinds of jobs. For him, music was music. It did not matter whether his audience was made up of gamblers or socialites.

Joplin made many friends and was a kind of leader to young musicians. Quiet and retiring, he developed a reputation for being a dedicated teacher. He wanted to help other African Americans to go beyond "Negro music" as a way of being accepted into the cultural mainstream. He roomed in Sedalia with the Marshall family, and Arthur Marshall, the son of Joplin's landlord, became a student and a friend of his. The Marshall family moved to Sedalia because their children could go to school for nine months a year there instead of the usual three months allowed blacks elsewhere. They also had heard that the townspeople of Sedalia were more accepting of African Americans.

Marshall later spoke about how kind and nurturing Joplin was to younger musicians. Joplin was 13 years older than Marshall, and 14 years older than the slender Scott Hayden, another student. Joplin eventually collaborated on pieces with both students.

Joplin finished the first draft of "Maple Leaf Rag" in 1897 or 1898 and took it to several publishers in Kansas City and Sedalia, including A. W. Perry & Son. He knew it was special, for he said to Marshall, "Arthur, the Maple Leaf will make me king of ragtime composers." To his great disappointment, the piece was continually turned down. He kept on playing it in various clubs and saloons, however, polishing it with every performance. Other ragtime pianists also began to play it, and the piece soon started to become popular in the area. "Maple Leaf Rag" was much more sophisticated and melodious than "Original Rags."

Finally, John Stark accepted it, and history was made. Many felt that Stark struck one of the bargains of the century, since sales of "Maple Leaf Rag" eventually made him a relatively wealthy man. The music business was not like it is today, however, when a new hit song can sell millions within months; but for the times, "Maple Leaf Rag" did well. The first year, it sold around 400 copies. By 1909, it had sold a half-million copies. Many orders came from the F. W. Woolworth chain of stores around the country. By 1909, Joplin's royalties amounted to $600 a year.

Joplin was so eager to have his music published that he probably would have agreed to a contract on almost any terms. And no one—including Stark or Joplin—could have known that the work would become so successful. In Stark's defense, he was a pioneer in offering a fair contract to a black musician, since many companies turned down composers because of their race. Stark would be well regarded by most black ragtime composers for the rest of his life, since he was one of the few publishers willing to give them a chance. It is important to remember that African Americans were working within a white system. They created the music, but white businessmen and musicians were the ones who introduced the music to the American population.

On the cover of the original version of "Maple Leaf Rag," which was first published in September 1899, is an illustration

Where "Maple Leaf Rag" Got Its Name

There has been much speculation over the years about where Scott Joplin got the name for "Maple Leaf Rag." The *Sedalia Times* said in 1903 that it was named after a club that Tony Williams opened in Sedalia. Tom Ireland, however, a colleague of Joplin's, claimed otherwise. He insisted that Williams had opened up a club room and called it the Maple Leaf Club after Joplin arranged his "Maple Leaf Rag." Experts are certain the rag had been written by 1898, while the Maple Leaf Club opened in November of that year.

Some people believe the term *maple leaf* refers to Canada, which has the maple leaf as its national symbol. Many slaves tried to escape to Canada, and so some speculate that the names of the song and the club refer to the black hope for freedom and equality.

Others say *maple leaf* is connected to the Chicago Great Western Railway route, known as the maple leaf route because it resembled the outline of a maple leaf. The railroad used the maple leaf in its advertising, which was printed in Sedalia newspapers in 1899. But was this the inspiration for the title?

Another possibility is found in the abundance of maple trees in Sedalia. The biggest house in town was called Maple Square, and a nearby community was called Maplewood. The word *leaf* was popular for no particular reason and was used in the names of other clubs, like the Clover Leaf Club and the Autumn Leaf Club.

African-American dancers performed the cakewalk dance at the Pan-American Exposition in Buffalo, New York. Ragtime was an ideal accompaniment for the cakewalk, because the dance was often improvised. The cakewalk dance had been around for years, but it became popular among the middle class in the mid-1890s.

of two black couples dressed in their finery, presumably on their way to a cakewalk dance—an indication of how closely tied ragtime was to the cakewalk fad. The word *cakewalk* comes from the contests held for performers of this dance. During such contests, the most skilled "walkers" competed for prizes, which sometimes included cakes. In the middle of the nineteenth century, the cakewalk was featured extensively on the minstrel stage. People from the middle class suddenly discovered the dance in the mid-1890s, and the cakewalk became an overnight sensation.

A TOUCH OF ACCLAIM

Joplin suddenly became something of a celebrity, as did the short-lived Maple Leaf Club. There were two black clubs in Sedalia, the Black 400 Club, and later, the Maple Leaf Club. A friend of Joplin's, Tony Williams, was an impresario and the most famous cakewalker in the Sedalia area. Members of white clubs who wanted to learn the cakewalk often hired him. In October 1898, Williams and his brother, Charles, opened a club

The Cakewalk

An important element in ragtime's rise in acceptance was the popularity of a ragtime-like dance, the cakewalk. Before this dance became popular, one of the dances performed most often in the 1890s was called the two-step, which was danced by couples, like a waltz. The two-step was basically a glorified march; it was danced to marches like Sousa's "Washington Post March" and "Stars and Stripes Forever." When dance bands and orchestras started to jazz up their march performances with the jauntier rhythms of ragtime, the dancers found that the livelier music did not affect their dancing, since they could still hear the steady march beat under the new and complex rhythm.

The cakewalk, which became popular in the mid-1890s, was a different kind of dance. It was also danced by couples, yet it featured high-stepping, prancing, and strutting. The dance form had originated among black slaves in the early part of the century. It may have originally been a parody of the formal dances done by whites who lived in plantation mansions. Ragtime music was the perfect accompaniment to the cakewalk, for the dance was not a set routine. Cakewalk dancers were supposed to improvise steps, struts, and kicks to fit the syncopation of the music. By 1898, cakewalk contests were regularly being held across the country as a part of social outings, especially on excursions and picnics.

called the Black 400, where admission was to be by card, or invitation, as they were determined to create a respectable place. Joplin and the Queen City Cornet Band played there on at least two occasions. Then, in November, the Maple Leaf Club was incorporated. Joplin, Marshall, and others played there. The club held dances, cakewalks, and masquerades attended by blacks and whites. Within a couple of months, the mayor shut down both clubs after a group of black pastors complained. The clubs reopened after the owners complained, but the ministers returned in force, claiming that the two clubs were "a detriment to the morals of our people." The dispute continued, and finally Tony Williams was arrested for serving liquor without a license. That same evening, the Black 400 Club held a masquerade ball, attended by many prominent whites who had come to support Williams.

After a trial, Williams and other members of the Black 400 Club were found not guilty of serving liquor without a license. Both clubs closed their doors for the summer, since the heat was too intense. By the fall of 1899, Williams had moved to Joplin, Missouri, and opened a club there. Someone else reopened the Black 400 Club. When the Maple Leaf Club reopened, Arthur Marshall got into a fight after he tried to steal someone's date, and a rumble occurred. The police shut the club down, and there was more trouble after it reopened again. Finally, the doors were permanently closed in January 1900. The name lived on, however, because of Joplin's song.

Pianists from all over Missouri came to Sedalia to compete against Joplin in ragtime contests, which Joplin would invariably win. The winner of a ragtime contest was decided by the audience at the competition, so even when other pianists brought their own cheering sections to Sedalia, Joplin's fans would easily outnumber and out-applaud them. Along with performing in Sedalia, Joplin continued to give a few performances on the road. In some of the towns in which he appeared, Maple Leaf Clubs were formed in his honor.

The ragtime fad was in full swing. Publishers from all over were suddenly printing anything that they could pass off as the new music. Even old pieces that did not have a hint of ragtime syncopation were rereleased, with new covers containing the magic word across the front: RAGTIME!

IMITATION RAGTIME

John Stark and Joplin made a distinction between musicians of classic ragtime and those who were commercial musicians, or imitators. Stark used the concept often in his advertising. Generally, it meant that Stark's musicians—namely Joplin, a white composer named Joseph Lamb, and James Scott—had an integrity and seriousness to their music that made it a classical art. In an advertisement in 1915, Stark wrote, "We are the storm center of high-class instrumental rags. The whole rag fabric of this country was built around our 'Maple Leaf,' 'Sunflower,' 'Cascades,' 'Entertainer,' etc."

As well as being a gifted salesman, Stark understood the value of "hype" in advertising. It was the new age of consumerism, and Stark never let an opportunity go by to promote his musicians. On the other hand, he was keen to separate the music he published from the less interesting rags, which were being published for a market looking for easy rags to play.

Joplin was composing in his free time. He collaborated on a song called "Swipesy Cake Walk" with Arthur Marshall, which was published by Stark in 1900. The original cover had small photographs of Joplin and Marshall on it, but later they were taken off, and only the picture of a black boy, "Swipesy," remained. The boy used to shine Stark's shoes, and Stark had him photographed. When he saw the picture, he thought the boy looked as if he had just stolen some cookies and decided to call the song "Swipesy."

Joplin was constantly revising the music that he submitted, as well as that of his students. In 1901, he collaborated with Scott Hayden on a piece called "Sunflower Slow Drag." Joplin was in love with Belle Hayden, the widow of Scott Hayden's older brother, and it seemed obvious to many who heard the song's lilting and haunting melody that it was the work of a man in love.

Sadly, some of the people Joplin worked with claimed that he had not written "Maple Leaf Rag" alone. Otis Saunders, who had been a close friend, tried to take credit for it, a move that ended the friendship. Saunders also said that he had composed Tom Turpin's song "St. Louis Rag," which suggests that he had a habit of spreading rumors about his role in the works of more successful composers. Later, Arthur Marshall's daughter stated that her father had composed "Maple Leaf Rag," but when he was interviewed, he had only good things to say about his friend. Marshall said that Joplin was "one of the most pleasant men you'd ever want to meet.... He was kind to all of us musicians.... He was an inspiration to us all."

A WEDDING

The turn of the century was a happy time for the serious Joplin—especially in his personal life. The musical collaboration between Joplin and Hayden that produced "Sunflower Slow Drag" had given Joplin an excellent opportunity to spend more time in the Hayden household and to get to know Belle. By late 1900, it was clear that although Belle did not share Joplin's passion for music, she loved him. They married soon after.

Not much later, Joplin met a man from St. Louis who would have a profound and far-reaching effect on his life. Alfred Ernst, the German-born director of the St. Louis Choral Symphony Society, visited Sedalia and got to know the 32-year-old ragtime composer. Ernst was quite taken with Joplin and his

Above, Stephanie and Jeremy Potter of Pueblo, Colorado, appear in the Turn of the Century Fashion Contest at the Scott Joplin Ragtime Festival in June 2005 in Sedalia, Missouri. Although Sedalia was Joplin's home for just a few short years, the town was where his career began to blossom. A connection between Joplin and Sedalia continues to this day. The Scott Joplin International Ragtime Foundation is based in Sedalia, and it holds a festival there each year.

music. In an interview published by the *St. Louis Post-Dispatch* in February 1901, Ernst said of him:

> I am deeply interested in this man. He is young and undoubtedly has a fine future. With proper cultivation, I believe, his talent will develop into positive genius. Being of African blood himself, Joplin has a keener insight into that peculiar branch of melody than white

composers. His ear is particularly acute.... The work Joplin has done in ragtime is so original, so distinctly individual, and so melodious withal, that I am led to believe he can do something fine in compositions of a higher class when he shall have been instructed in theory and harmony.... The soul of a composer is there [in Joplin's work] and needs but to be set free by knowledge of techniques. He is an unusually intelligent young man and fairly well educated.

Such words from a European-trained classical musician pleased Joplin. They were also an encouragement to a young composer whose main desire was to have his music taken seriously. Ragtime, as popular as it was, was still relegated to the lower ranks of the music world. Musical theater was where Joplin now wanted to make his mark. Ernst offered to take on Joplin as a student, and Joplin agreed. In early 1901, Joplin and his wife moved to St. Louis, where Ernst lived. John Stark and his family had also moved to St. Louis, establishing his music company there. This was probably the happiest time in Joplin's life. He was composing works like "The Entertainer" (1902) that leading piano players and orchestras were performing. He was being written up regularly in newspapers in Sedalia and St. Louis.

Joplin could look back one day and see how he and the town of Sedalia had had a profound impact on each other. He had been given great freedom and encouragement to pursue his music there. What he did not realize was that there would be many social and cultural barriers for him and his peers once they left the town that had nurtured them.

5

King of Ragtime

Scott Joplin's move to St. Louis in 1901 felt like a homecoming. His brother Robert was living in the city, and within the year their brother Will joined them there. Also in St. Louis were Joplin's old friends, the Turpins. Scott Hayden had recently married, and he and his bride also decided to make their home in St. Louis. They moved into the same row of houses as the Joplins. Other musicians from Sedalia—including Otis Saunders, who was touring with McCabe's Minstrel Troupe as a singer, and Arthur Marshall—visited Joplin frequently. Both Hayden and Marshall considered Joplin a mentor. John Stark had settled there the year before, and over the next few years, many other musicians would leave Sedalia for St. Louis.

Joplin listed himself in the St. Louis city directory simply as "Joplin, Scott, music." Although his rags were not simplified, the demand for them continued. To combat the commercialization of ragtime, he deliberately wrote rags that were more serious in nature and that were to be played slower than the mass-produced rags. This did not seem to hurt his popularity, however. In fact, from 1901 to 1903, he had 16 pieces published. They were "Peacherine Rag," "The Augustan Club," "The Easy Winners," "Cleopha," "A Breeze From Alabama," "Elite Syncopations," "March Majestic," "The Strenuous Life," "Weeping Willow," "Palm Leaf Rag," "I Am Thinking of My Pickaninny Days," "Little Black Baby," "The Ragtime Dance," "Something Doing," "Sunflower Slow Drag," and "The Entertainer."

PATTERN OF THE RAGS

Joplin used the same formula for most of his rags. "The Entertainer" offers a good example of his work. The song, which was used in the 1973 movie *The Sting*, is probably his best-known piece today. It starts off with a brief introduction, which is followed by the first section (called the chorus), consisting of an upbeat melody. The second section is in the same key but has a different melody, which is something of an elaboration of the melody of the chorus but often is more complex and exciting. After this, the first section (chorus) is played again. For the third section, the composition changes to another key and introduces a third melody. This is followed by a short four-measure "bridge," which serves as a transition from the key of the third section back to the original key. The final section, which is played in the original key, has a closing melody that brings the piece to its conclusion.

All of Joplin's rags are sectional. Like "The Entertainer," they have several distinct segments, with each segment having a different melody. A performer usually plays each melody twice before moving to the next section. The opening melody, or chorus, is almost always repeated after one or two of the new melodies are played.

The challenging commercial aspects of the music business back then are hard to imagine today. Rags were written for

"The Entertainer," which was composed in 1902, is probably the best known of Scott Joplin's works. It was featured in *The Sting*, a 1973 film that won the Oscar for best picture. "The Entertainer," like most of Joplin's rags, has distinct segments, with each having a different melody.

piano, which was the most popular musical instrument in America. Until the middle of the nineteenth century, pianos belonged mostly to wealthy white Americans. The upright piano was invented in 1800 by a man named John Isaac Hawkins. After the 1820s, new technological innovations made pianos much more affordable. By 1900, 150,000 pianos were being made; soon after, piano companies merged, and prices fell considerably. The competition was fierce. In Sedalia, for example, in the mid-1890s, when John Stark owned a music store, he was competing with several other stores. He added a tremendous stock of sheet music to attract more buyers to his store.

The number of pianos sold in the United States at the turn of the twentieth century was phenomenal. Much of this rise in sales was because of the new popular music, ragtime and the like, although some people were sad to see the classics being replaced by what they thought of as recklessness. The piano was contributing to an entertainment industry that consisted of concerts by celebrities and vaudeville.

The ragtime pieces were much more difficult to play than the standard popular pieces of sheet music. The tricky ragtime rhythm was the stumbling block. In ragtime, there is always a steady beat in the bass, which is played by the pianist with his left hand. The right hand plays the melody. The strong accents in the melody are placed so that they deliberately fall on the weak beats established by the steady rhythm of the left hand. This rhythm technique is known as syncopation; the parts of the melody that are stressed fall in places where someone normally does not hear an accented sound. It is precisely this juxtaposition of the right-hand melody (with its "wrong" accents) against the steady beat played by the left hand that creates the "ragged time."

Over the years, syncopated rhythms have become common in jazz and rock music, which are in part outgrowths of ragtime. Yet before ragtime, very little popular music in the United States incorporated such complex rhythms. To American listeners and piano players back then, ragtime's rhythms were entirely new, somewhat mysterious, and devilishly hard to master.

The arrangers who worked for the major New York music publishers, which printed much of the country's sheet music,

A young woman in Georgia is shown receiving a piano lesson in this photograph from 1899 or 1900. Back then, the piano was the most popular musical instrument in the United States, and the new music—ragtime and the like—contributed to the rise in piano sales.

also had trouble at first determining how to write down the complex rhythms they heard when ragtime performers played. As the public began to clamor for ragtime music, however, these arrangers managed to figure out how to write down the rags. Publishers also hired ragtime composers and performers to write simple pieces so that lesser-skilled piano players could play the music. Because these pieces were playable, they sold well, thus fueling the ragtime craze even more. The commercial musical establishment was soon cranking out hundreds of ragtime compositions. Since the upright pianos in the publishers' showrooms had basically a tinny sound, the area in New York City where most of the ragtime publishers were based soon became known as Tin Pan Alley.

WORKING WITH STARK

For the most part, Joplin's working arrangement with John Stark was harmonious and beneficial to both parties. Most of their disagreements stemmed from Joplin's intense desire to be considered a serious composer. He was interested in elevating ragtime from the realm of popular music to the realm of serious art. Stark was not as interested in elevating music—he was interested in selling it. After all, he was a businessman. Joplin generally kept to his agreement with Stark. There were times, however, when the composer had disagreements with Stark and believed that the publisher was not treating him fairly. When such conflicts surfaced, Joplin took his work to another publisher, perhaps to show Stark that he did not have complete control over Joplin.

Joplin felt that if he worked hard enough, he could single-handedly elevate ragtime music; not only for his own benefit, but for the benefit of other black musicians—for ragtime was the music of much of black America. Joplin had decided he would not limit his compositions to the short piano rags he apparently could write with ease. Several months before Stark published "Maple Leaf Rag," Joplin started to compose the music for a larger work: a dramatic ragtime folk ballet. The form was his own creation, and the idea was a startling one.

Joplin's ballet, called *The Ragtime Dance*, was based on black social dances of the era. He wrote the words and the music to the work and indicated which dances were to be performed. These included the ragtime dance, the cakewalk prance, the clean-up dance, the dude walk, the stop-time dance, the Jennie Cooler dance, the slow drag, and the back-step prance. The ballet has a vocal introduction, followed by the dances, which are directed by the vocalist. Joplin's associates and friends in Sedalia, including his brother Will and Arthur Marshall, encouraged him to work on *The Ragtime Dance* and helped him by copying out parts for the various instruments in the orchestra. Once the ballet was completed, Joplin formed the Scott Joplin Drama Company. In late 1899, he rented the Woods Opera House in Sedalia for a single performance—one performance of the ballet was all he could afford to produce. He invited everyone he knew, including the Stark family, who he hoped could be persuaded to publish the lengthy work.

The performance was a success with Joplin's friends and acquaintances. But Stark was not interested in publishing the work. He pointed out that the ballet was too long and too difficult to play. Besides, who would buy it? As a businessman, Stark understood the odds against such a work becoming popular. Yet Joplin felt that the publisher was being excessively cautious and was impeding his artistic development. In Stark's defense, the ballet was performed before the phenomenal success of "Maple Leaf Rag," so Joplin had not yet proved that his work would sell.

When Joplin moved to St. Louis, he continued to work on *The Ragtime Dance*. It is likely that he showed it to Alfred Ernst for his assessment. In late 1901, Joplin mounted another production of the ballet, this time solely for the Stark family. Stark's daughter Nell, who had recently returned from Europe, where she had been studying music, was in the audience. She enjoyed the ballet and tried to persuade her father to publish it. Stark, though, remained unenthusiastic. Angry at Stark's refusal to publish the ballet, Joplin decided to publish one of his rags, "The Easy Winners," on his own. The sheet music boasted on the cover: "Composed by Scott Joplin: King of Ragtime Writers." He also took several other rags to different publishers.

In 1902, Stark reluctantly gave in to Joplin's demands—perhaps because he felt he owed something to the composer. After all, "Maple Leaf Rag" had made him a successful businessman. Ignoring his good business sense, Stark agreed to publish all nine pages of *The Ragtime Dance*.

Joplin was greatly encouraged. His compositions were selling well, and he believed that *The Ragtime Dance* would finally be recognized as a major work. An article in the *Sedalia Times* referred to him as the "Rag Time King," and the editor wrote that Joplin's compositions were "used by the leading players and orchestras." Furthermore, according to the article, he spent his time "writing, composing, and collecting his money from the different music houses in St. Louis, Chicago, New York and a number of other cities"—a rather enviable existence, although not quite an accurate description of Joplin's real life. The *St. Louis Globe-Democrat* also carried a biographical article. "Despite the ebony hue of his features and a retiring disposition," it reported, Joplin "has written probably more instrumental successes than any other local composer." The author also pointed out that Joplin was known as "The King of Rag Time Writers" because of "the many famous works in syncopated melodies which he has written."

A GUEST OF HONOR

Joplin and his wife soon moved to a larger apartment, where he started to work feverishly on yet another serious and large composition, a ragtime opera called *A Guest of Honor*, based on President Theodore Roosevelt's invitation in 1901 to black leader Booker T. Washington for dinner at the White House.

Booker T. Washington (above), the political leader and educator, was one of the most influential African-American figures in the early 1900s. Scott Joplin wrote his first ragtime opera, *A Guest of Honor*, based on President Theodore Roosevelt's invitation to Washington to have dinner at the White House. *A Guest of Honor* was presented in St. Louis in August 1903 to favorable audience response, but a touring production proved to be ill-fated.

The invitation upset many white people, who worried that the dinner symbolized social equality between whites and blacks. To Joplin's great disappointment, Stark was not interested in publishing the work. His business sense about *The Ragtime Dance* had been correct, and the ballet had not sold well. People wanted rags they could sing or play on their parlor pianos. They did not want to buy a ragtime ballet or opera. Stark was not at all interested in sinking more time and money into another large, serious musical work that the ragtime-buying public would ignore.

Joplin continued to study with Alfred Ernst while teaching several of his own students. His seriousness and devotion to music attracted a large number of pupils. They considered him a teacher, a mentor, and a hero. In retrospect, this is not surprising. Although Joplin was quiet, he was friendly and supportive, and he formed lasting friendships easily. In addition, he had a personality that many people found irresistible. Perhaps his quietness made the dynamic side of his personality seem all the more forceful. He possessed the will and the determination to make something of himself, to have his music and the music of his people accepted by American society. All of these personality traits earned him the respect of his peers, along with the respect of the young musicians who sought to emulate him.

In March 1902, Joplin revived the Scott Joplin Drama Company and began to rehearse his one-act opera, which featured 12 ragtime numbers. Marshall and Hayden were members of the troupe, which Joplin soon decided to call the Scott Joplin Ragtime Opera Company.

PROBLEMS AT HOME

Musically, it was a creative time, but trouble was brewing at home. Joplin's work on *A Guest of Honor* took up more and more of his time. And Belle, who did not understand his preoccupation with music, started to feel ignored and abandoned by him. Marshall later described the problems that the couple had by saying: "Mrs. Joplin wasn't so interested in music, and her taking violin lessons from Scott was a perfect failure. Mr. Joplin was seriously humiliated. Of course unpleasant attitudes and lack of home interests occurred between them.... [Joplin] told me his wife had no interest in his musical career." The family discord disturbed Joplin's concentration, and his work began to suffer, which must have made him even more impatient and irritable with Belle.

In late 1902, Belle announced that she was expecting a child. She and her husband were happy with this new development, hopeful that a baby would help draw them back together. But their hopes were ill-founded. The child, a girl, was born sickly and lived for only a few months. Belle became despondent after the baby's death, and she and Joplin decided in mid-1903 to separate. Belle moved to Chicago and remained there until she died in 1930. Joplin sold their home to Marshall and moved in with the Turpins for a short while.

Joplin continued to write and teach. His growing fame as "The Ragtime King," however, was beginning to be a problem. Because Joplin was the "King," he was challenged more than ever before to play in ragtime competitions. In these contests, which were judged by the audience, two pianists would compete by playing faster and increasingly complex versions of the same tune. Although Joplin preferred to spend his time composing rather than playing, his many years as a performer—as well as his pride in his skill, ability, and experience—would not allow him to ignore these challenges.

Ragtime performances, though, had changed since Joplin had given up steady performing. The preferred performance style had become flashier, more technically demanding, and faster. Joplin's style of playing, like all of his rags, was still lyrical, slow, and serious. Determined to elevate ragtime to a more dignified musical form, he was not interested in the flashy and less serious style of the newer rags. All of his rags had begun to appear with the instruction "Not Fast."

Consequently, Joplin's playing style was not flashy or fast enough to impress the new ragtime audiences. His classic rags and his sober style of performing were no longer appreciated as much as they had been. Accordingly, he began to play less often in public. He refused to play for people who were not interested in his style of music; after all, he was a classic ragtime composer.

A Guest of Honor was presented in August 1903 in a large dance hall in St. Louis, and the audience's reaction was favorable. The production also attracted the attention of two major booking agencies in town, Majestic and Haviland. Both wanted to promote a touring production of the opera. Joplin decided to take the Scott Joplin Ragtime Opera Company and *A Guest of Honor* on the road.

A TOUR IN TROUBLE

The company had 12 members when it left St. Louis in the fall of 1903. At first the tour went well. Joplin was received as a celebrity in the saloons and cafes of the small towns in the Midwest. There he was able to play his works in his own style; he was able to forget about the flashy and rapid-fire playing of the hotshot St. Louis performers. The company performed in Nebraska, Iowa, and Missouri, and may have also gone to Illinois and Kentucky. The tour, though, started to run into trouble after a month on the road. Perhaps some personality conflicts arose between members of the company or the performances displeased the composer for some reason. Then someone in the company stole the box office receipts, which left Joplin unable to meet his expenses. One story is that the opera score was confiscated at a boardinghouse in Kansas to pay the bill, but Joplin claimed that the trunk that contained the manuscript was stolen.

Joplin had applied for a copyright for the opera in early 1903, but no manuscript of the work was ever sent to the U.S. Copyright Office in Washington, D.C. All copies of the opera have subsequently been lost. Today, the whereabouts of *A Guest of Honor* continue to tantalize any scholar or music lover who has ever been interested in Scott Joplin. Although Stark had expressed mild interest in acquiring *A Guest of Honor*, those hopes were dashed.

At least five members left the company after the first month of the tour. The remaining seven members pooled their abilities and past performance experience and formed a minstrel show, which was booked into various theaters and halls in Missouri, Nebraska, and Iowa in September and October 1903. This company, however, collapsed as well.

A discouraged Joplin prepared to return to St. Louis. When he arrived there, he was greeted with a parade. The residents of Chestnut Valley had apparently heard of his arrival and had decided they were not going to let their favorite ragtime composer return to St. Louis feeling as if he were a failure. They hoped to show their support and lift his spirits with the parade. Despite this welcome, he stayed in St. Louis only briefly.

With the collapse of his marriage and the failure of his first opera, Joplin felt that he was losing his concentration. The past months, which had been filled with anger, tension, and unhappiness, had left him upset. He had been on top of the world only a short time before. He had thought that his days of wandering were over. Now St. Louis was just a town full of bad memories. He decided to hit the road again.

6

Life on the Road

The next two-and-a-half years were very difficult for Scott Joplin. He returned to St. Louis in 1904. Tony Williams, who had owned the black clubs in Sedalia, was there, managing a cafe on Market Street that featured music and dance. Tom Turpin owned the Rosebud Café, where he was sponsoring a contest between the brilliant, young Louis Chauvin and himself. They were considered the two best pianists in St. Louis. Chauvin came in first.

Early in 1904, Joplin went to Arkansas to visit relatives. Freddie Alexander, who lived in Little Rock, was 19 when Joplin fell in love with her. He was 36, though he claimed he was 27, probably because of their age difference. She was a strong proponent of racial pride and their African-American heritage. He wrote a rag, "The Chrysanthemum: An Afro-American Intermezzo," and dedicated it to her.

Cavalry soldiers marched through the grounds at the St. Louis World's Fair in 1904. Scott Joplin's rag "The Cascades" was written to commemorate the fair's Cascade Gardens, with its fountains and lagoons. The song was one of the hits at the fair.

The St. Louis World's Fair started on April 30, 1904. The official name was the Louisiana Purchase Exposition. Blacks were urged by the editors of African-American newspapers to refuse to attend because of discrimination, but many went anyhow. It must have felt discouraging for blacks, for the decade between the Chicago World's Fair and the St. Louis World's Fair had not produced much change in race relations.

One big difference, though, was that Joplin's rag, "The Cascades," was one of the hits at the St. Louis fair. It was written to commemorate the beautiful Cascade Gardens, a huge complex of fountains, pools, lagoons, and ponds that served as the main concourse during the fair. John Stark wrote, "Hear it, and you can fairly feel the earth wave under your feet. It is as high-class as Chopin and is creating a great sensation among musicians."

HEARTACHE

Joplin played in a band in St. Louis led by a man named Samuel Joseph Reed, and he also began to seek new publishers for his work, as his five-year contract with Stark had ended. He and Freddie were married in June 1904 in Little Rock, Arkansas, and from there they went to Sedalia. Joplin started giving performances. Freddie became ill with a cold, which soon turned into pneumonia. Her sister came to stay with her, but she died on September 10, only 10 weeks after she and Joplin were married. It was a terrible shock that left Joplin devastated.

His whereabouts after that are not known until he showed up in early 1905 in St. Louis, where he reconnected with Tom Turpin. Another young ragtime artist, James Scott, went in search of Joplin, who subsequently introduced Scott to John Stark. Over the next 16 years, Stark published many of the new composer's rags. Stark moved to New York and left his son, William, to manage the office in St. Louis. Stark published Joplin's piece "The Rosebud March," which referred to Turpin's saloon. "The Maple Leaf Rag" continued to do well. It was performed on a regular basis by the U.S. Marine Band. In 1905, the president's daughter, Alice Roosevelt, was a fan. A member of the Marine Band recalled:

> Miss Roosevelt came up [at a White House reception) and said, "Oh, Mr. Santelmann, do play the 'Maple Leaf Rag' for me…" "'The Maple Leaf Rag?'" he gasped in astonishment. "Indeed, Miss Roosevelt, I've never heard of such a composition, and I'm sure it's not in our library." "Now, now, Mr. Santelmann," laughed Alice. "Don't tell me that. The band boys have played it

Alice Roosevelt, the flamboyant daughter of President Theodore Roosevelt, was a fan of Scott Joplin's music. During one function at the White House, she asked the U.S. Marine Band to play "Maple Leaf Rag."

for me time and again when Mr. Smith or Mr. Van-poucke was conducting, and I'll wager they all know it without the music."

LIFE IN CHICAGO

In 1905, Joplin headed to Chicago, where he stayed with Arthur Marshall and his wife. He became reacquainted with several younger musicians he had known in the past. With Marshall as a collaborator, he wrote "The Lily Queen." And with the help of Louis Chauvin, he wrote a work entitled "Heliotrope Bouquet."

Working with Chauvin was ultimately discouraging, for the younger musician represented the underside of life as an itinerant musician. Chauvin was only 19 when he first met Joplin, shortly after Joplin and his wife moved to St. Louis. Chauvin quickly became a part of Joplin's circle of friends. It was obvious that he had talent and much promise as a pianist and a composer. Unfortunately, he loved the fast life of the red-light district and was unwilling to give it up. When Joplin met him in Chicago, Chauvin was paying the price for living a fast life. Addicted to opium, he was usually so high on the drug that he could not concentrate on what he was doing. Although he was blessed with the ability to write beautiful melodies, he did not have the concentration or the discipline to finish anything. Fragments of his melodies lay around his residence, written on scraps of paper.

Joplin was shocked and saddened when he saw what had become of Chauvin. He took two of the younger man's beautiful themes, added two of his own, and put them together to create "Heliotrope Bouquet." Although Chauvin and Joplin worked together for a while on the piece, Joplin did most of the polishing since Chauvin had difficulty concentrating on their work. Stark published "Heliotrope Bouquet," an instrumental piece, in 1907, only a year before Chauvin died from syphilis at the age of 27.

Chauvin's fate was not an unusual one for musicians whose principal places of employment were in the sporting districts

of large cities. It was difficult to resist the dangerous tempta-
tions in such areas—difficult especially for a young and imma-
ture musician.

The waste of Chauvin's talent reinforced Joplin's determination to make ragtime music respectable, but he was continuing
to find it difficult to concentrate. After staying with the Mar-
shalls for a short while, he moved to a boardinghouse. But
before long, in 1906, he left Chicago and resumed the life of a
wandering performer. He traveled around the Midwest, playing
wherever he was offered work. In 1907, he found himself back
near his hometown, Texarkana, Texas. He decided to visit the
members of his family who still lived there. His mother died
some years earlier, but his father was still in town, living with
Joplin's older brother, Monroe, and his family.

Joplin received a rousing welcome from the black community in Texarkana. He was a local boy who had overcome his
impoverished beginnings and had become a success. His name
was known all over the country, and his music could be found
propped up on the pianos in most of the parlors in America.
Joplin's homecoming was especially exciting for his family.
They kept him up for most of the night after he arrived, talking and reminiscing. Long after midnight, Joplin played some
of his pieces for his family on the piano. "I heard the music,
and I got out of bed and just sat there, listening," his nephew
Fred Joplin recalled.

During Joplin's visit, he taught his young niece Nettie how
to play "Maple Leaf Rag." He also did some entertaining
around town. After staying for a few days, he went back to St.
Louis, never to return to his Texas hometown. Joplin settled
down once more in St. Louis. Over the last few years, his rate
of composition had fallen off drastically. He published only
three works in 1906, his least productive year since 1901. He
must have been profoundly discouraged.

ON TO NEW YORK

Later in 1907, Joplin decided to visit John Stark, who had moved his offices to New York City. For years, Joplin had wanted to go to New York. This seemed to be as good a time as any. During the early 1900s, New York was becoming one of the most heavily populated black urban areas in the United States. A large number of blacks were leaving the rural South for greater job opportunities in the industrial North. Among these migrants were black musicians and entertainers eager to become a part of New York's growing black community.

At the time, more than 100 publishers in New York City were competing with one another in the lucrative ragtime market. Most of them were located in Tin Pan Alley, an area on 28th Street between 5th Avenue and Broadway. After arriving in New York, Joplin caught some of the sense of optimism that was in the air, and he started to perform and compose again. In 1907, he published eight works—a large increase over his

Vaudeville

When Scott Joplin joined the vaudeville circuit, he did so during the heyday of this form of entertainment. Vaudeville was most popular from the 1880s to the 1920s. Similar to a variety show, vaudeville featured an array of performers with a range of talents. At a typical show, there could be music, comedy, acrobats, Shakespeare, and lectures by celebrities and intellectuals.

One difference between vaudeville and earlier types of variety entertainment was its mixed-gender audience and its appeal to the middle class. That meant nothing offensive was to be performed—instead, there were to be polite acts that appealed to men, women, and children. Of course, some performers flouted such restrictions.

Vaudeville's rise came in conjunction with the growth of American cities. The introduction of radio and cinema helped bring about its gradual decline a few decades later. Still, many vaudevillians were able to carve out new careers in radio and film. They included W. C. Fields, the Marx Brothers, the Three Stooges, and Judy Garland. Later, the influence of vaudeville could be seen in the variety shows that became popular on television.

output just a year before. Some of his outstanding rags from this period are "Rose Leaf Rag" and "Pine Apple Rag."

Joplin also signed up to tour on the vaudeville circuit. He spent the next several years on the road billed as "The King of Ragtime Composers—the Author of Maple Leaf Rag." On the vaudeville circuit, he performed in theaters and halls rather than in honky-tonks and saloons. He was also able to perform in his own slow and smooth style. He was still battling against the pianists who were mainly interested in playing ragtime as fast as they could. They did not seem to care whether they were playing the right notes or rhythms. Joplin's earnest attitude managed to show through in his performances. Instead of acting like a vaudeville performer, he presented the image of a serious musician.

During this tour, Joplin traveled all over the Midwest and up and down the East Coast. On a visit to Washington, D.C., in 1907, he met 33-year-old Lottie Stokes. They fell in love and were soon married. Lottie began to travel with Joplin on his tours. Lottie's attitude toward his music was the opposite of that of his first wife, Belle. Lottie loved his music and was enthusiastic about all of his projects and dreams. In time, she would prove to be his fiercest defender and supporter. The love and support that Lottie gave Joplin meant a great deal to him. For the first time in years, he began to look to the future with confidence and anticipation.

7

The Ragtime Controversy

The Tenderloin district of New York City was filled with saloons, theaters, gambling houses, and brothels. It was known for corruption. The name *Tenderloin* came about in the late 1870s when a police captain named Alexander C. Williams was transferred to the area. While before he had eaten chuck steak, Williams said, in this precinct he dined on tenderloin steak— that is, he earned enough in bribe money to afford better meat. This area was also the theater district, part of which would eventually become Broadway. On the theater scene, a black musical called *In Dahomey* had already been a big success by the time Scott Joplin arrived in New York. Other musicals soon followed, some composed by Joplin's friends.

During the first decade of the twentieth century, most of the well-crafted, high-quality rags were forced off the market by simpler, less interesting rags, which were published for a market seeking easy rags to play. Most amateur pianists did not

Above is a scene from the musical *In Dahomey*, which debuted in 1903, and already was a success by the time Scott Joplin arrived in New York. *In Dahomey* was the first Broadway musical to star and be written by African Americans. It was popular with audiences of all races.

recognize the difference between the commercialized rags printed by Tin Pan Alley publishers and the classic rags of Joplin and those who were influenced by him.

A TRAINING MANUAL

Joplin understood that an amateur pianist could have trouble playing his complicated rhythms. He believed, however, that the solution was not to simplify the rags but to train the pianists correctly. To help their training, he wrote a ragtime instruction manual, *School of Ragtime*. It consisted of a set of six exercises designed to assist pianists having trouble with the complicated rhythms of ragtime. Originally published in 1908, *School of Ragtime* was the first book on ragtime published by a black American. A ragtime instruction manual written by a white ragtime pianist had been published in 1897.

In his preface to *School of Ragtime*, Joplin denounced the trashy commercial pieces that were "masquerading under the name of ragtime." These pieces, he wrote, were "not the genuine article." He also attacked the type of ragtime performance that emphasized speed. In the directions to the first exercise in his book, Joplin wrote, "Never play ragtime fast at any time." By then, of course, these instructions had become something of a motto for him.

The controversy surrounding ragtime concerned more than just its often-frenzied performance style. It seemed to Joplin that the harder he struggled to have ragtime recognized by the musical establishment, the more difficult that struggle became. For much of the public in the early part of the twentieth century, ragtime was associated with "coon songs," not piano works. One writer in 1901 sputtered with indignation that "this cheap, trashy stuff could not elevate even the most degraded minds, nor could it possibly urge anyone to greater effort in the acquisition of culture in any phase." A writer in the *Negro Music Journal* in 1902 sought to rally the anti-ragtime troops by saying: "Let us take a united stand against the *Ragtime Evil* as we would against bad

IN HIS OWN WORDS...

Scott Joplin did not like what many so-called musicians were doing to ragtime once it had become a popular form of music. He believed in a ragtime of a higher class, and he took every opportunity to convince people of its musical veracity. In *School of Ragtime*, the manual he wrote, he said:

What is scurrilously called ragtime is an invention that is here to stay.... That all publications masquerading under the name of ragtime are not the genuine article will be better known when these exercises are studied. That real ragtime of the higher class is rather difficult to play is a painful truth which most pianists have discovered. Syncopations are no indication of light or trashy music, and to shy bricks at "hateful ragtime" no longer passes for musical culture. To assist amateur players in giving the "Joplin Rags" that weird and intoxicating effect intended by the composer is the object of this work.

literature, and horrors of war or intemperance and other socially destructive evils."

By 1910, the attacks on ragtime in newspapers, magazines, books, and pamphlets were coming faster than ever. With most of the classical musical establishment opposed to ragtime, the period was a discouraging one for Joplin and other lovers of high-quality ragtime music.

RAGTIME'S OPPOSITION

There were several reasons for all of the opposition to ragtime. The first was the growing distinction between classical music and popular music. Many music educators believed that it was necessary to teach Americans how to listen to and perform higher forms of music. Because ragtime was so incredibly popular, it represented a serious threat to the efforts of these classical music lovers to elevate the musical tastes of most Americans. As early as 1899, the music magazine *Etude* was warning:

> Pass along the streets of any large city on a summer evening when the windows are open and take note of what music you hear being played. It is no longer the great masters, or the lesser classicists—nor even the "Salon-componisten" that used to be prime favorites with the boarding-school misses. Not a bit of it! It is "rag-time."

Ragtime was described in magazine articles as a "ragweed of music" and "a poison that destroys the musical tastes of the young." Besides the highbrows concerned with musical taste, there were also many people deeply worried about decaying morals, especially of the young. These people were quick to point out that ragtime had originated in honky-tonks, saloons, and other places of ill repute. It was obvious, they argued, that any musical style with its origins in such places had to be bad, even if it was played on a parlor piano. They believed that ragtime would inevitably lower moral standards. These same opponents of ragtime also decided that because it was so popular, it must be addictive or have unknown, mysterious powers.

Etude in 1900 called ragtime a "virulent poison" and pointed out that it was "finding its way into the homes and the brains of the youth to such an extent as to arouse one's suspicions of their sanity." Others claimed that ragtime's extensive use of syncopation would cause permanent brain damage and harm the nervous systems of listeners and performers.

Much of the moral criticism of ragtime and many of the suspicions about it and its origins were, in fact, poorly disguised excuses for racism. The United States was a highly segregated society, and many white Americans felt threatened by this musical form, not only because it had been developed by black Americans but also because it incorporated strong elements of African and Afro-American rhythms. Ragtime opponents believed that the words to ragtime songs, the melodies of ragtime pieces, and the unconventional rhythms were indecent. A writer for *Ladies' Home Journal* said that "jazz originally was the accompaniment of the voodoo dancer, stimulating the half-crazed barbarians to the vilest deeds. The weird chant, accompanied by the syncopated rhythm of the voodoo invokers, has been employed by other barbaric people to stimulate brutality and sensuality."

Curiously, whites accepted African-American folk music, like spirituals and plantation chants, because it was safe. According to Matthew Mooney, writing for *Americana: The Journal of American Pop Culture,* "it [folk music] represented a time when Blacks 'knew their place' at the bottom of the social hierarchy under slavery."

A STRUGGLE FOR LEGITIMACY

Joplin's fight to legitimize ragtime was, to a large extent, a fight to legitimize the music of black Americans. His fight, though, was not universally accepted. African Americans were divided when it came to their loyalty to ragtime. Middle-class blacks, especially in the cities, were struggling for respect in a white man's world. They longed for social equality. Part of the way they tried to integrate was to dismiss the music from their past, and to adopt the more sedate, classical music so favored by upper-class whites. They joined in the outcry against ragtime. In their defense, they had concerns that the mass-marketed popular music was reinforcing racist stereotypes. In their minds, ragtime was associated with minstrels and "coon songs."

One of the odder aspects of the resistance to ragtime was that both the modern thinkers and the traditional thinkers agreed that the music was aimed at the body, rather than the intellect. Writers started describing the unsettling effect that the music had on its listeners. In 1903, a music professor said, "Suddenly I discovered that my legs were in a condition of

IN HIS OWN WORDS...

The shame that many African Americans had about ragtime being a creation of their race was painful to Scott Joplin. According to Edward A. Berlin, Joplin explained his viewpoint to *New York Age* reporter Lester A. Walton:

> I have often sat in theaters and listened to beautiful ragtime melodies set to almost vulgar words as a song, and I have wondered why some composers will continue to make the public hate ragtime melodies because the melodies are set to such bad words.
>
> I have often heard people say after they had heard a ragtime song, "I like the music, but I don't like the words." ... If someone were to put vulgar words to a strain of one of Beethoven's beautiful symphonies, people would begin saying, "I don't like Beethoven's symphonies."
>
> Ragtime rhythm is a syncopation original with the colored people, though many of them are ashamed of it. But the other races throughout the world are learning to write and make use of ragtime melodies. It is the rage in England today. When composers put decent words to ragtime melodies, there will be very little kicking from the public about ragtime.

The Czech composer Antonín Dvořák (above) was enthusiastic about the black-influenced music that was being performed in the United States around the turn of the twentieth century. "These beautiful and varied themes are the product of the soil. They are American," Dvořák said.

great excitement. They twitched as though charged with electricity and betrayed a considerable and rather dangerous desire to jerk me from my seat."

This statement makes us laugh today, but back then much was written about the mystery of the sway the music had. A conductor visiting from Poland said, "Day and night you Americans tingle tangle and jingle jangle ragtime band stuff with [dances like the] grizzly bear, tom cat, and turkey trot. This is not music; this is madness. Awful. Terrible." Other critics felt that this kind of dancing made people mentally unstable. Some magazines went as far as to claim that there was scientific proof to that effect.

A famous European composer, Antonin Dvořák, to whom Joplin was compared by a white reviewer, remained enthusiastic about the expressive American music. In 1893 during a stay in the United States, he wrote, "I am now satisfied that the future music of this country must be founded upon what are called the Negro melodies. This must be the real foundation of any serious and original school of composition to be developed in the United States.... These beautiful and varied themes are the product of the soil. They are American."

For the modern thinkers, popular music mimicked the bustling cities. It reflected the creative, industrialized energy of urban places. Consumer goods were multiplying daily, and people could not seem to get enough. Though the traditionalists hoped they could return to more civil times, the speed of entertainment and living continued to ratchet up as jazz became popular. An observer in 1920 said that "the jazz was simply ragtime speeded up and raised to the nth degree."

8

Treemonisha—An Opera

It is easy to see how Scott Joplin might have become discouraged. But even though his dream of turning ragtime into a respected art form sometimes seemed to be an impossible one, he refused to give up. As John Stark had discovered when Joplin tried to get him to publish *The Ragtime Dance*, Joplin could be a very stubborn man. He refused to simplify his rags. In fact, after 1905, he almost always included the following instruction in the left-hand corner of his compositions: "*NOTICE!*: Do not play this piece fast. It is never right to play ragtime fast. The Composer."

In his continuing struggle, Joplin had one staunch supporter: John Stark. After settling in New York City, Stark had refused to publish the unrefined yet popular commercial pieces that other publishers were turning out daily. He remained loyal to Joplin and his serious and artistic rags. Stark even paid for large advertisements in the musical press to support serious ragtime, and he sometimes ridiculed the anti-ragtime snobbery of those who promoted classical music. His advertisement for Joplin's "The Cascades" is a good example of his marketing campaign. Stark wrote:

A FIERCE TRAGEDY IN ONE ACT

SCENE: A Fashionable Theatre. Enter Mrs. Van Clausenberg and party—late, of course.

MRS. VAN C.: What is the orchestra playing? It is the grandest thing I have ever heard. It is positively inspiring.

YOUNG AMERICA (in the seat behind): Why, that is "The Cascades" by Scott Joplin.

MRS. VAN C.: Well, that is one on me. I thought I had heard all of the great music, but this is the most thrilling piece I have ever heard. I suppose Joplin is a Pole who was educated in Paris.

YOUNG AM.: Not so you could notice it. He's a young Negro from Texarkana, and the piece they are playing is a rag.

Sensations—Perturbation—Trepidation—and Seven Other Kinds of Emotion.

MRS. VAN C.: #%&'$@ The idea! The very word ragtime rasps my finer sensibilities. (*Rising*) I'm going home, and I'll never come to this theatre again. I just can't stand trashy music.

Yet Stark's loyalty to Joplin had a price. Stark's faith in serious ragtime caused him financial difficulties. The Tin Pan Alley publishers had begun to consolidate into larger companies, which reduced the price of their music, undercutting the competition. Stark was caught in a bind. Not only were the rags that he published not as popular as the others, but he also had to charge more for them. He began to lose business fast. And to make matters worse, his wife became seriously ill.

A SPLIT WITH STARK

Stark refused to publish Joplin's new opera. To improve his financial situation, he suggested to Joplin in 1909 that they give up the royalty arrangement they had always used in the past. Instead, Stark wanted to purchase the composer's pieces outright for a specific sum of money. Joplin was outraged at this suggestion. He considered Stark's plan to be an insult, and he refused. Joplin argued that publishers usually purchased pieces outright only from struggling young composers—not from composers who were as well known and as well established as he was. Joplin had had enough. He refused to publish with Stark after that. The long-standing and mutually beneficial association that had existed between Joplin and Stark for more than 10 years came to an end.

Joseph Lamb, a white ragtime pianist of note, collaborated with Joplin on a rag, and when Lamb took the piece to Stark, Stark said that he would only publish it if Joplin's name was taken off of it. Lamb would not agree, and that piece of music was lost.

Joplin went on to publish with Seminary Music, the first piece being "Sugar Cane." He may have been playing at the historic Fraunces Tavern in New York at that time. Seminary was part of a trio of music companies (the others being Crown Music and Ted Snyder Music) that became a legend. In 1909, Ted Snyder hired a young genius lyricist named Irving Berlin, whose life would cross with Joplin's.

Over the years, Joplin had become increasingly convinced that there was only one way to win the support and respect of the established music community, which seemed prepared to condemn all forms of ragtime—even Joplin's serious classical rags. He had never given up on his dream of producing a

To Scott Joplin (above), there was only one way to win the respect of the established music community, which seemed to look down on all forms of ragtime. Joplin believed that he needed to produce a serious, large-scale musical work.

successful, large-scale musical work. The shows on Broadway offered encouragement. Musical theater had become distinctly American instead of British. Most important, black musical

comedies were starting to be produced. A landmark show entitled *A Trip to Coontown*, with an all-black cast, opened off-
Broadway in 1898. The unfortunate title was a spoof on a
popular show on Broadway called *A Trip to Chinatown*. Other
African-American shows opened months later.

Joplin had been discouraged by his inability to get *A Guest of
Honor* published. He still believed, however, that a large-scale
work was the correct route to his gaining acceptance. It was up
to him to write a work of such stellar quality that the musical
establishment would be forced to sit up and take notice.

A NEW, SERIOUS WORK

Back when Joplin was living in St. Louis, he had started to work
on another large musical composition besides *A Guest of Honor*.
He had continued to work on the composition off and on for
several years. His life on the vaudeville circuit greatly inter-
rupted his composing, making it almost impossible for him to
find long stretches of uninterrupted time in which to write.

By 1907, he had completed enough of the large-scale work
to be able to play parts of it for friends in Washington, D.C. By
1908, he had a finished draft. The opera that would occupy his
mind for the next decade was called *Treemonisha*.

A black newspaper writer named Lester A. Walton was a
strong supporter of African-American musical dramatic
endeavors, and he must have learned of Joplin's ambitious
opera. He wrote in March 1908,

> From ragtime to grand opera is certainly a big jump—
> about as great a jump as from the American Theatre to
> the Manhattan and Metropolitan Opera Houses. Yet
> we believe that the time is not far off when America
> will produce several S. [Samuel] Coleridge Taylors
> who will prove to the public that the black man can
> compose other than ragtime music.

Out of economic necessity, Joplin continued to travel and
perform during 1910. Despite the distractions and disruptions

DID YOU KNOW?

Everyone knows that the *Titanic* passenger ship sank on April 15, 1912, killing more than 1,500 people. In the ongoing controversy over what the final song played was—in James Cameron's 1997 film *Titanic*, the band played the hymn "Nearer, My God, to Thee"—what rarely emerges is that survivors recalled hearing ragtime songs before the ship went down. Some had specific memories of hearing "Alexander's Ragtime Band" and "Oh, You Beautiful Doll." Notes from the University of San Diego History Department's Website state that before the ship sailed, the *Titanic*'s bandleader, Wallace Hartley, was asked by a reporter what he would play in the event of a disaster. He replied that he would play "cheerful stuff, such as ragtime."

He explained to fellow musician Lewis Cross when asked what music he would use if there was a shipwreck: "Well, I don't suppose it will ever happen, but you know music is a bigger weapon than a gun in a big emergency, and I think that a band could do more to calm passengers than all the officers."

A passenger named Mrs. Gold, who was one of the last to leave the ship, was quoted as saying, "When we left the ship, men were sitting on A deck, smoking cigarettes and tapping time with their feet to the music of the band. These passengers and the bandsmen, too, had their lifebelts beside them, and I was specially struck by a glimpse of a violinist playing steadily with a great lifebelt in front of him. The music was ragtime just then."

Another passenger, Mrs. Paul Schabert, recalled that after playing ragtime, the band switched to hymns. And as for the final song? The controversy continues to this day, with the two top contenders being the somber "Nearer, My God, to Thee" and "Songe d'Automne," a popular waltz. Most researchers, though, agree that "Nearer, My God, to Thee" was the last song played, as it was reportedly Hartley's favorite hymn.

Authors John P. Eaton and Charles A. Haas, who wrote *Titanic: Destination Disaster*, thought the argument irrelevant: "The musicians stayed until all hope of rescue was gone. Who can say how many lives their efforts saved? The final moments of how many were cheered or ennobled by their music? What difference [the songs]? The memory of the bandsmen and their courageous music will never die."

of his hectic schedule, he managed to finish a second draft of *Treemonisha* by the end of the year. The following year, he and his wife rented some rooms in a boarding house on West 47th Street in New York. Joplin gave up performing on the vaudeville circuit and instead earned a living by teaching a few students. Most of his time and energy, however, went to working on the opera. He had almost completely given up writing ragtime piano pieces; in 1910, he published only two works, and he would publish only one ragtime piece in 1911 and one in 1912.

There was no extra money in the Joplin household, but they had friendship and good times. The home on 47th Street was in an area of New York where many musicians and actors lived. The Joplins' rooms were often filled with people who were also entertainers.

Located just a block from Broadway, the main street in New York's theater district, the Joplin home was not too far from Tin Pan Alley. The nearby streets were lined with the shops of music publishers. Once Joplin felt that he was more or less finished with his opera, he tried to find a publisher. Day after day, he went from company to company with the manuscript of the opera in hand. No one was the least bit interested in publishing it. Although Joplin became discouraged, he was determined that *Treemonisha* would not suffer the same fate as *A Guest of Honor* had.

After months of rejection, Joplin decided to give up on the New York publishers and publish *Treemonisha* himself. He somehow managed to scrape together enough money to pay for a printer. The manuscript first appeared in May 1911, under his own imprint: Scott Joplin Music Pub. Co., New York City, NY.

A GRAND OPERA IN THREE ACTS

The score to *Treemonisha* is 230 pages long. The work is a grand opera in three acts, complete with an orchestral

The music publishing house of Leo Feist was one of many on
West 28th Street in New York City, the area known as Tin
Pan Alley. Scott Joplin shopped his ambitious folk opera
Treemonisha around to all the publishers on Tin Pan Alley.
None of them wanted to purchase it, so Joplin decided to
publish it on his own.

overture and instrumental preludes to the second and third
acts. There are 27 musical numbers in the opera, including
recitatives (sung dialogue), arias (songs), and choruses. There

are also several dances, to which Joplin choreographed the steps. In *Treemonisha*, he synthesized all the ragtime forms he had developed over the years. In some of the pieces, he integrated the rag style in a subtle fashion. The overall work, though, is not a ragtime opera, for only three of the numbers are obviously and unmistakably ragtime in style. In fact, Joplin called *Treemonisha* a folk opera.

The opera's plot is rather simple, but the underlying message is one that had been of vital importance to Joplin for most of his life. The story is set in Arkansas, near Texarkana, in 1884. The main characters—all black—are former slaves who have been left to fend for themselves in the years after the Civil War. They are simple people who live in ignorance and believe in superstition and conjuring. Because of their superstitions, it has been easy for conjurers to cheat them out of their money by selling them "bags of luck."

Treemonisha is the main character in the opera. Her mother's name is Monisha, and as a child, the girl loved to sit under a particular tree—hence her name, Treemonisha. Her parents arrange for her to be educated, and the opera commences when Treemonisha is 18 and has just started her career as a teacher and leader of her people. The plot revolves around the conflict between Treemonisha and the neighborhood conjurer, who knows he will lose his livelihood once the people have been educated and are no longer superstitious. By the end of the opera, Treemonisha outsmarts the conjurer, and knowledge triumphs over ignorance. The opera's message—that education is the salvation of black people in the United States—was close to Joplin's heart.

Soon after Joplin published the opera, a rave review appeared in the June 1911 issue of *American Musician and Art Journal*, praising him as

> a teacher as well as a scholar and an optimist with a mission.... [He] has created an original type of music in which he employs syncopation in a most artistic and

original manner.... Moreover, he has created an entirely new phase of musical art and has produced a thoroughly American opera.

These kind words helped Joplin feel as if his music had finally been recognized for what it was: original, artistic, and truly American.

Armed with copies of the review, Joplin set off in search of backers for a production of *Treemonisha*. He placed notices in local newspapers and knocked on the doors of dozens of potential producers. The lack of interest was disappointing. In August 1913, however, a notice appeared in *New York Age* announcing that the opera would be produced that fall at the Lafayette Theatre in Harlem. Joplin was overjoyed and immediately advertised for singers. But the production soon fell through, and Joplin slid into a deep depression.

9

Joplin's Last Years

In late 1913, Scott Joplin managed to pull himself out of his depression and wrote one of his last rags, "Magnetic Rag," which was published the following year. He was low on money and hoped to earn some income from the royalties. He also advertised for more students. To save rent money, he and Lottie moved from 47th Street to a building on West 138th Street in Harlem, which was quickly becoming one of the most heavily populated black areas in New York. Joplin advertised himself as a teacher. His ad read: "Scott Joplin, the composer, has moved from 252 West 47th Street to 133 West 138th Street. He will devote a part of his time to the instruction of pupils on the violin and piano." The financial situation must have been desperate. At the end of 1914, he was trying to sell his music through the mail.

Sam Patterson, a former student of Joplin's from St. Louis, arrived in New York around this time and volunteered to help the composer with his opera. The instrumental part of *Treemonisha* had been written for the piano only. Joplin had planned to stage a performance of the opera himself with the hope of attracting backers. It was a tremendous job to transform the music for the piano into music for various instruments of the orchestra. Joplin and Patterson worked day and night on the orchestration.

A PRODUCTION OF *TREEMONISHA*

In early 1915, Joplin rented the Lincoln Theatre on 135th Street in Harlem for a performance of *Treemonisha*. He gathered together a group of singers and dancers who probably worked for little or no pay. Joplin worked hard at rehearsing the cast and hammering the opera into shape. Despite all of the long hours that he and Patterson had put into orchestrating the opera, it soon became apparent that there was no money to hire an orchestra. At the first performance of

Piano Rolls

Piano rolls, which were first mass-produced beginning in 1897, are used with player pianos, among other instruments. A player piano is a type of piano that plays automatically. The piano rolls are rolls of paper with holes punched in them. The position and length of each hole determine the note played on the piano. The piano roll moves over a "tracker bar," which has 88 holes for each piano key.

Scott Joplin made seven hand-played piano rolls in the spring of 1916. The piano hammers marked a roll as the performer played. The technical person would then use the marks as a guide for punching holes in the master roll. The QRS Piano Roll Company issued a Joplin song called "Silver Swan Rag" in 1914. Another company called the National Music Roll Company also issued it. QRS listed seven Joplin pieces in its catalog. They were "Original Rags," "Maple Leaf Rag," "Swipesy Cake Walk," "The Easy Winners," "The Entertainer," "Palm Leaf Rag," "March and Two Step," and "A Princeton Tiger," which turned out not to be composed by Joplin but by a man named Gerald Burke.

J. Lawrence Cook, who was known as the dean of piano-roll arrangers around 1950, examined perforated sheets he had just completed. The position of the perforated holes on the rolls determines the notes played on the piano.

Treemonisha, Joplin himself ended up playing all of the music on the piano. Likewise, there was no money for costumes or scenery, so the production was rather bleak. Confident of the power of his music, Joplin hoped that the opera would succeed on the basis of the music and the dancing.

He was wrong. The audience, which consisted mostly of friends, was small. Their applause was polite but not enthusiastic. The lukewarm reception was not what Joplin had hoped to hear. Probably what was most disappointing was that there was no support from the cultural and intellectual leaders of Harlem. They were more interested in advanced education and professional training. Northerners by birth, they did not relate to the Southern oppression of blacks, the superstitions of Southern blacks, and the complete lack of literacy. Joplin was simply unable to penetrate that circle.

Even if *Treemonisha* had been splendidly mounted, complete with costumes, scenery, and a full orchestra, it probably would not have succeeded. The opera's subject matter was too close to home for many black Americans in 1915. They did not want to be reminded of life on plantations in the South, where ignorance and superstition were commonplace. They were eager to put their unpleasant history behind them. Even worse than the polite reaction of the audience was that of the musical press: virtual silence. For Joplin, the failure of *Treemonisha* meant the end of a life's worth of dreams and hopes. He had been in failing health for some time, experiencing the physical and mental effects of syphilis, but his obsession with the opera had given him the strength to press on and to ignore his physical problems. The opera's failure was a blow from which he would not recover.

Joplin announced two new works in 1915. One was called "Morning Glories," and the other was a vaudeville act that was called "The Syncopated Jamboree." The former was never completed, and "Jamboree" was never performed.

ILLNESS

Eubie Blake, who was in the next generation of famous ragtimers after Joplin and his fellow musicians, met Joplin in 1915 at a reception in Washington, D.C. Many ragtime pianists were

**Eubie Blake (above), among the next generation of ragtime com-
posers, met Scott Joplin at a reception in 1915. It was apparent
to Blake that Joplin was suffering the effects of syphilis.**

there, and some played. They asked Joplin to perform. At first
he said no, but finally he agreed. He played "Maple Leaf Rag."
Blake said, "So pitiful. He was so far gone with the dog
[syphilis], and he sounded like a little child tryin' to pick out a
tune.... I hated to see him tryin' so hard. He was so weak. He
was dead, but he was breathing. I went to see him after, but he
could hardly speak he was so ill."

In 1916, Joplin told friends that he was working on a musical comedy entitled *If* and a piece named Symphony No. 1, which he called a "great ragtime number." He announced he was going to his sister's home to recuperate from a serious illness. He was suffering from syphilis, a sexually transmitted disease. Usually, the effects of the disease are felt 20 or so years after the disease is contracted. It causes mental and physical deterioration. Eventually the patient becomes paralyzed and dies. Joplin surely knew what was wrong with him, for many of his friends had died from the same disease, including Louis Chauvin.

Joplin seemed to have a classic case. He had loss of memory and irritability. Then he went through a manic-depressive stage, where he suffered extreme highs and lows. This was followed by slurring in his speech and an inability to complete sentences. By late 1916, he started to act paranoid. He thought that people were stealing music from him. Near the beginning of 1917, he destroyed many of the musical sketches and unfinished pieces that were on his desk. He still had lucid periods, but they were becoming less and less frequent.

On February 3, 1917, he was admitted to the Manhattan State Hospital on Ward's Island. He soon became paralyzed and could not even recognize the friends who came to visit him. The March 29 issue of the *New York Age* had the following notice: "Scott Joplin, composer of the 'Maple Leaf Rag' and other syncopated melodies, is a patient at Ward's Island for mental trouble." Three days later, on April 1, 1917, he died. The cause of his death was "dementia paralytica-cerebral," with contributing complications from syphilis, although his wife would later comment, "You might say he died of disappointment, his health broken mentally and physically."

Only two newspapers mentioned his death. Lester Walton wrote in the *New York Age*, "Scott Joplin, known throughout the United States as the composer of syncopated music, died Sunday at the Manhattan State Hospital, where he had been confined for a number of months for mental trouble."

A funeral for Joplin was held on April 5, 1917. John Stark gave a brief, touching eulogy. He said, "Scott Joplin is dead. A homeless itinerant, he left his mark on American music." When he had learned that Joplin had died, Stark decided to publish the piece called "Reflection Rag," which Joplin had handed to him just before their split.

Joplin was buried in a common grave in St. Michael's Cemetery in the Astoria section of Queens, New York. Joplin had made a request years before that "Maple Leaf Rag" be played at his funeral. When Lottie was making the arrangements, however, she decided that it would not be appropriate to play that work at a funeral. Yet she later regretted this decision, saying, "How many, many times since then I've wished to my heart that I'd said yes."

Music publisher Edward B. Marks said, "Joplin's was a curious story. His compositions became more and more intricate, until they were almost jazz Bach. 'Boy,' he used to tell the other colored song writers, 'when I'm dead 25 years, people are going to begin to recognize me.'"

10

A Glorious Legacy

Ragtime did not die with Scott Joplin in 1917, but it almost did. The incredible popularity of the music in the first years after 1900 was over. The fickle American public embraced it for a short time, then forgot it. The Original Dixieland Jazz Band opened in New York in January 1917 and took the city by storm, much as ragtime had more than a decade earlier. Rags were still published on occasion, but the interest in the musical form was waning. By the time that Joplin's friend Tom Turpin died in 1922, the days of ragtime were finished. The American public, in the midst of the Roaring Twenties, had a new musical style to call its own: jazz. It sprang from the ragtime of Scott Joplin and his followers, as well as from the syncopated music of New Orleans, which was different in spirit and in musical form. Jelly Roll Morton became famous for his songs. Other kinds of music were developing at the same time as ragtime. Blues for example, was a form of music that started in the South and was making its way into the American consciousness.

RAGTIME'S EBB

Joplin was not completely forgotten, however. A handful of people, like his wife, Lottie, and an old friend, S. Brunson Campbell, tried to promote ragtime. But their efforts, for the most part, were unsuccessful. Ragtime was dead.

In 1936, the African-American scholar Alain Locke wrote about piano ragtime in his book *The Negro and His Music.* He was dismissive about ragtime piano. He called it thin, with a "rather superficial eccentric rhythm." He did, however, include Joplin by saying that "a few artists like the famous Scott Joplin wrote real rag in compositions like his 'Maple Leaf Rag' (1899) and 'Palm Leaf Rag' (1903)."

Locke also mentioned the song that the whole country found captivating: "Alexander's Ragtime Band," by Irving Berlin. Joplin claimed that Berlin had stolen the song from him, and in fact, members of the Stark family confirmed it. The story in Joplin's family was that Joplin had taken his song to Berlin, who kept it for a long time. Berlin was working at the time at Joplin's publisher, Crown-Seminary-Snyder. When Joplin went back, Berlin said he couldn't use it. When "Alexander's Ragtime Band" was released, Joplin said, "That's my tune." The Starks said that when Joplin heard Berlin's song, which would become a big hit, he started to cry. Joplin's song, the finale to *Treemononisha,* was called "A Real Slow Drag." Joplin claimed that Berlin had used music from the "Marching On" section of the finale, and he decided—or was forced—to change his song in *Treemonisha.* Berlin denied that he had stolen the song.

As early as 1907, Claude Debussy in Paris, France, wrote *Golliwog's Cakewalk.* Other modern classical composers who incorporated ragged rhythms in their work included Erik Satie, Igor Stravinsky, and Paul Hindemith.

"Maple Leaf Rag" was never out of print. Nine recordings of it were made in the 1920s, with still more in the 1930s. John

"Alexander's Ragtime Band" by Irving Berlin was popular across the nation after it came out in 1911. Scott Joplin claimed that Berlin stole the song from him—that it had been part of his folk opera *Treemonisha*. Berlin denied that he lifted the tune.

Stark continued to publish it, averaging 5,000 copies a month into the 1920s.

Lottie Joplin had started a rooming house on West 131st Street when she and Joplin were poor, and she continued to take in boarders from the entertainment world. Jelly Roll Morton stayed there, as did jazz pianist Willie "The Lion" Smith. He said that it was not unusual to "step in at six in the morning and see guys like Eubie Blake, Jimmy Johnson … sitting around talking or playing the piano in the parlor." He said that they would play "Maple Leaf Rag" for Lottie.

Swing bands came into popularity in the 1930s and 1940s. Count Basie, Duke Ellington, and Benny Goodman were but a few of the musicians that became household names. More and more musicians wanted to go back to the more traditional styles. Piano ragtime was making a comeback. In 1945, a magazine called *The Record Changer* published a number of articles on Joplin. In 1950, Rudi Blesh and Harriet Janis wrote *They All Played Ragtime*, a wonderful biography of Joplin and the history of that era. Alan Lomax's biography of Jelly Roll Morton was published that same year.

In 1965, the director of the Utah State University opera company put excerpts from *Treemonisha* into a program along with Bach's *Magnificat*. By then, interest in ragtime had also grown stronger. A magazine called *Rag Times*—featuring the motto "Scott Joplin Lives!"—was started in California in 1966. Soon after, a pianist and music historian named Joshua Rifkin, who was studying ragtime as a forerunner of jazz, realized that ragtime compositions were very interesting themselves. In 1970, he released a ragtime recording, *Piano Rags by Scott Joplin*, that immediately became a hit.

A RESOUNDING REVIVAL

In the mid-1970s, the name *Scott Joplin* and the word *ragtime* finally became widely known again throughout America. George Roy Hill, a Hollywood film director, heard one of Rifkin's ragtime recordings and decided that ragtime music would serve as an ideal soundtrack for the movie he was making. The movie was *The Sting*, starring Robert Redford and Paul Newman.

Hill and composer Marvin Hamlisch selected a number of Joplin's rags—including "Gladiolus Rag," "Pine Apple Rag," "Solace," "The Ragtime Dance," and "The Entertainer"—to use on the soundtrack. Not only did *The Sting* go on to win the

Robert Redford (left) and Paul Newman appear in *The Sting*. The film used several of Scott Joplin's songs on its sound-track, and the movie's score won an Oscar. *The Sting* also helped fuel a resurgent interest in ragtime and in Joplin's career and works.

Academy Award for Best Picture in 1974, but the score also won an Oscar. By the fall of 1974, the soundtrack for *The Sting* had sold over two million copies. America was once again listening to Joplin's music.

Official recognition for Joplin soon followed. The residents of Sedalia started the Scott Joplin International Ragtime Foundation, and a memorial plaque was erected on the site of the old Maple Leaf Club in honor of Joplin and Stark. The Scott Joplin Ragtime Festival was organized in Sedalia in 1974, and revived in 1983. The people of Texarkana held a Scott Joplin Centennial Concert, during which his rags were played and members of his family were honored.

And *Treemonisha* was finally produced—first in Atlanta, next in Washington, D.C., and then in Houston, Texas. In 1975, a dream of Joplin's came true: *Treemonisha* opened before a packed audience on Broadway in New York. The crowd loved it.

A year later, Joplin posthumously received a Pulitzer Prize. The prize was awarded to honor his lifetime of work as a composer of ragtime music. Joplin once commented that his music would not be appreciated until 25 years after his death. His estimation was not wrong by very much.

THE MAN AND HIS MUSIC

Joplin was a man who knew what he wanted and who was willing to work hard to fulfill his dreams. Lottie Joplin said of him,

> He was a great man, a *great* man! He wanted to be a real leader. He wanted to free his people from poverty, ignorance, and superstition, just like the heroine of his ragtime opera, *Treemonisha*. That's why he was so ambitious; that's why he tackled major projects. In fact, that's why he was so far ahead of his time.

Today Scott Joplin's influence is still very much with us. He and Tom Turpin were the first to make ragtime a household word, and they were followed by James Scott, Louis Chauvin, Arthur Marshall, Scott Hayden, Tony Jackson, and Jelly Roll Morton. Another kind of ragtime followed, led by Eubie Blake, Willie "The Lion" Smith, Fats Waller, and others. They played against the grain, as it were, for tremendous criticism was aimed at their music. But they paved the way for the many African Americans in the music world today who are the creators and producers of a variety of genres of music.

Joplin has been honored for his music, but his life also had meaning. His place in the history of American music is secure—thanks to his foresight, musical genius, and simple hard work.

Compositions by Scott Joplin

1895 "A Picture of Her Face"; "Please Say You Will"

1896 "Combination March"; "The Great Crush Collision March"; "Harmony Club Waltz"

1899 "Maple Leaf Rag"; "Original Rags" (arranged by Charles N. Daniels)

1900 "Swipesy Cake Walk"

1901 "The Augustan Club"; "The Easy Winners"; "Peacherine Rag"; "Sunflower Slow Drag"

1902 "A Breeze From Alabama"; "Cleopha"; "Elite Syncopations"; "The Entertainer"; "I Am Thinking of My Pickaninny Days"; "March Majestic"; "The Ragtime Dance"; "The Strenuous Life"

1903 "Little Black Baby"; "Palm Leaf Rag"; "Something Doing"; "Weeping Willow"; "A Guest of Honor"

1904 "The Cascades"; "The Sycamore"; "The Chrysanthemum"; "The Favorite"

1905 "Bethena"; "The Rosebud March"; "Binks' Waltz"; "Leola"; "Sarah Dear" (words by Henry Jackson); "You Stand Good With Me, Babe" (lost)

1906 "Antoinette"; "Eugenia"; "Good-Bye Old Gal Good-Bye"

1907 "Gladiolus Rag"; "Lily Queen"; "Heliotrope Bouquet" (with Louis Chauvin); "The Nonpareil"; "Rose Leaf Rag"; "Searchlight Rag"; "Snoring Sampson" (by Harry La Mertha; arranged by Scott Joplin); "When Your Hair Is Like the Snow" (words by Owen Spendthrift)

1908 "Fig Leaf Rag"; "Pine Apple Rag"; "School of Ragtime—6 Exercises for Piano"; "Sensation" (by Joseph F. Lamb; arranged by Scott Joplin); "Sugar Cane"

1909 "Country Club"; "Paragon Rag"; "Euphonic Sounds"; "Pleasant Moments"; "Solace"; "Wall Street Rag"

1910 "Stoptime Rag"

1911 "Felicity Rag"; "Lovin' Babe"; *Treemonisha*

1912 "Scott Joplin's New Rag"

1913 "Kismet Rag" (with Scott Hayden); "A Real Slow Drag" (*Treemonisha* excerpt); "Prelude to Act 3" (*Treemonisha* excerpt)

1914 "Magnetic Rag"; "Silver Swan Rag"

1915 "Frolic of the Bears" (*Treemonisha* excerpt); "Morning Glories" (lost); "The Syncopated Jamboree" (lost); "Pretty Pansy" (lost); "Recitative Rag" (lost); "For the Sake of All" (lost); "If," (lost); "Symphony No. 1" (lost); "Piano Concerto" (lost)

1917 "Reflection Rag"

Circa 1868 Born Scott Joplin in northeastern Texas

Mid-1880s Leaves home in Texarkana, Texas; becomes itinerant musician

1893 Visits World's Columbian Exposition in Chicago, Illinois

1894 Settles in Sedalia, Missouri; becomes member of the Queen City Cornet Band; tours with the Texas Medley Quartette

1895 Publishes first two songs, "Please Say You Will" and "A Picture of Her Face"

1897 Friend Tom Turpin becomes first black ragtime musician to be published, with "Harlem Rag"; Joplin likely finishes the first draft of "Maple Leaf Rag"

1898 Maple Leaf Club opens in Sedalia

1899 "Original Rags" and "Maple Leaf Rag" are published; forms the Scott Joplin Drama Company; a single performance of his folk ballet, *The Ragtime Dance*, is presented

1900 Marries Belle Hayden; meets Alfred Ernst, who becomes a mentor

1901 Moves to St. Louis; continues as Ernst's student

1902 "The Entertainer" is published; completes *A Guest of Honor*; John Stark agrees to publish *The Ragtime Dance*

1903 Joplin and his wife, Belle, separate; *A Guest of Honor* is produced in St. Louis; Joplin takes it on the road

1904 Attends St. Louis World's Fair; "The Cascades" is a big hit; marries Freddie Alexander and they return to Sedalia; she becomes ill and dies 10 weeks later

1905 Moves to Chicago

1907 Visits Texarkana; moves to New York; tours on vaudeville circuit; marries Lottie Stokes

1908 *School of Ragtime* is published

1909 End of friendship with his publisher John Stark

1911 Publishes *Treemonisha* on his own

1913 Writes "Magnetic Rags"

1915 Produces *Treemonisha*

1917 Enters Manhattan State Hospital in New York; dies on April 1

Berlin, Edward A. *Ragtime: A Musical and Cultural History*. Berkeley, Calif.: University of California Press, 1980.

Berlin, Edward A., *King of Ragtime: Scott Joplin and His Era*. New York and Oxford: Oxford University Press, 1994.

Blesh, Rudi, and Harriet Janis. *They All Played Ragtime*. New York: Oak Publications, 1971.

Curtis, Susan. *Dancing to a Black Man's Tune: A Life of Scott Joplin*. Columbia, Mo., and London: University of Missouri Press, 1994.

Haskins, James, and Kathleen Benson. *Scott Joplin*. Garden City, N.Y.: Doubleday, 1978.

Reed, Addison W. "Scott Joplin, Pioneer." In *Ragtime: Its History, Composers, and Music*, John Edward Hasse, ed. New York: Schirmer Books, 1985, pp. 117–136.

WEBSITES

Americana: The Journal of American Popular Culture, "An 'Invasion of Vulgarity': American Popular Music and Modernity in Press Media Discourse, 1900-1925"
www.americanpopularculture.com/journal/articles/spring_2004/mooney.htm

The Dee Family's Scott Joplin Sheet Music Collection
www.foxhanger.com/joplin/index.html

Edward A. Berlin's Website of Ragtime and Scholarship
www.edwardaberlin.com/

"Music That Americans Loved 100 Years Ago"
www.garlic.com/%7Etgracyk/century.htm

"Perfessor" Bill Edwards Ragtime Site
www.perfessorbill.com

The Scott Joplin International Ragtime Foundation
www.scottjoplin.org

Werner Icking Music Archive: Scott Joplin
http://icking-music-archive.org/ByComposer/Joplin.html

Picture Credits

page:

Janet Hubbard-Brown has written numerous biographies for children and young adults, the most recent of which are *Chaucer: Celebrated Poet and Author, Hernando de Soto and His Expeditions Across the Americas,* and *The Labonte Brothers.* She is a regular contributor to *Vermont Magazine.* She also teaches fiction, and is a freelance editor in Fayston, Vermont.